The Philosophy Of Existentialism

The Philosophy Of Existentialism

ADRIAN VAN KAAM'S EXISTENTIAL COUNSELING

Ernesto Logarta

ISBN: Softcover 978-1-4415-1915-3

This book was printed in the United States of America.

To order additional copies of this book, contact:
Xlibris Corporation
1-888-795-4274
www.Xlibris.com
Orders@Xlibris.com

60359

CONTENTS

***Dedicated to my wife, Cena
My two children,
Edmund
And
Ayn-lin

CHAPTER I

INTRODUCTION

We should not quarrel about definition, for there are many definitions of counseling as there are many kinds and types of counselors. The definition and importance of counseling would depend upon the philosophy of the particular counselor. This writer contends that counseling is a relationship in which the counselor helps the counselee to accept what he is and what he can become.

If one accepts this definition it follows that the importance of counseling is to assist an individual to develop the right attitude towards himself, a kind of proper love for oneself to be able to love his neighbor. In order to achieve self-actualization one must be able to become "a being for others." By being for others it means we serve those who are in need of our assistance, those who cry for our help, for our presence, for our availability and dialogue. It does not mean we learn to love oneself and others because society has conditioned us to do so. Counseling should be able to give us the insight that when we learn to love the self and serve others it is because we have freely chosen it to be the task of our existence that can give us meaning. Counseling does not teach us to adjust to society, for that would make us robots and automations; neither does it teach us to fight society. The importance of counseling is to lead us to the realization that loving oneself and others is the ultimate meaning of existence. It is to have an attitude built towards self-understanding whereby the individual can live in any society, be it democratic or not.

Thus, counseling is an attitude of spiritual freedom for oneself and others regardless of circumstances, situations, and outer restrictions.

In this thesis the writer will also make a distinction between techniques of counseling and the schools of psychotherapy. Techniques or approaches in counseling are the methods and procedures used by counselors from the initial interview to the termination of the counseling relationship resulting in the resolution of the conflict or attainment of the cure on the part of the client. Counselors may come from different backgrounds and orientations and theoretical allegiance but they all make use of one of the three techniques or a combination of the three, namely the directive, non-directive, and the eclectic approaches. Techniques in counseling should also be distinguished from the means of counseling. The means of counseling are the different instruments or strategies at the disposal of the counselor to probe, to detect the flaws in the personality of the client which is the source of the conflict. Examples of the means used by different counselors are the sentence completion test, the word test, the ink blot projections, dream analysis, and free association.

The different schools of psychotherapy differ from the techniques of counseling in the sense that the former is the theoretical construct of the personality. Every school of psychotherapy theorizes about human behavior and explains reality according to its own system or frame of reference. Freud explains the reality of man in terms of the pleasure principle while Adler in terms of will to power, and Frankl in terms of will to meaning. These different theories reinforce the techniques of counseling especially in their interpretation of the client's source of trouble or conflict.

The main concern of the thesis writer is the evaluation of a suggested counseling technique based on Adrian Van Kaam's existential counseling. There are various forms of counseling or psychotherapy such as: marriage counseling, psychiatric therapy, and psychological therapy. Wherever and whenever counseling is practiced and whatever form it appears as listed above, the writer contends that the existential counseling of Van Kaam is an attitude, an orientation of "authentic therapeutic care" which is applicable to all forms of counseling. In this research, the subjects to whom it is applied are college students.

THE PROBLEM

Statement of the Problem. This study aims to analyze Adrian Van Kaam's counseling techniques and its implications to counseling college students. Specifically, this study seeks to answer the following questions:

1. What are the important features of existential counseling techniques?
2. How do these features compare with the features of other existential philosophy?
3. What is the relevance of Adrian Van Kaam's Existential Counseling to counseling college students?

DEFINITION OF TERMS

Counseling and psychotherapy. This term is used to describe a specialized field of study which enables a man to help his fellowmen to remove obstacles and blocks which hinder them from being open to reality.[1]

Eclectic. It is the combination of the directive and non-directive approaches in which the counselor integrates the various methods and procedures and creates his own synthesis.[2]

Ego. A reality principle which guides the individual in adjusting to his environment.[3]

Existentialism.[4] A philosophy which developed after the outbreak of two world wars, World War I and II. This philosophy is free from any structure or system which characterized the traditional philosophizing. The existentialist philosopher is a man who solves his problems as he comes to confront them in his own concrete flesh and blood situation. There are no set standards or values prescribed by this new orientation or outlook. In man himself must he look for the values or standard as embodied in his basic existential structure; only then can man speak of values or standard.

There are representatives from diverse philosophies whose intellectual framework is basically existentialist. Marxists, Christians, Atheists, artists, and scientists are at home in existentialism.

---

1 Adrian Van Kaam, *The Art of Existential Counseling* (Pennsylvania: Dimension Books, 1966), pp. 16-17.

2 I. D. Chaplain, *Dictionary of Psychology* (New York: Dell Publishing Company, Inc., 1973, p. 152.

3 *Ibid.*, p. 137

4 *Ibid.*, p. 171.

Existential Analysis. A school of psychology which developed its own comprehensive—theoretical framework from the conclusions and generalizations of various schools of psychology and which borrowed concepts from theologies and philosophies to create a partial and provisional theoretical unity based on man's existence.[5]

Directive Counseling. A technique of counseling which is counselor-oriented and involves direction and guidance function.[6]

Homeostasis. A term used by Frankl to describe a tensionless state in the psychological order.[7]

Logotherapy. A school of psychotherapy which is concerned with man's existence and his search for meaning.[8]

Libido. A psychic energy which is the cause of the man's needs, drives, urges, instincts, etc.[9]

Id. The physical aspect of the human organism and its inherited traits and characteristics.[10]

Nondirective. A client-centered technique of counseling which allows the individual the choice and decision of his direction.[11]

Noodynamics. The theory that man needs conflict and tension to maintain inner equilibrium.[12]

---

5 *Ibid.*, p. 170.

6 *Ibid.*, p. 171.

7 *Ibid.*, p. 220.

8 Victor Frankl, *Man's Search for Meaning* (New York: Pocket Books, 1974), pp. 152-153.

9 Chaplain, *op. cit.*, p. 228.

10 *Ibid.*, p. 228.

11 *Ibid.*, p. 323.

12 Frankl, op. cit., p. 133.

Phenomenology.[13] The term derived from Greek words *phainomenon* and *logos*, the former means that which appears; the latter, *logos*, means words, science, or study of words. Therefore phenomenology is a study of that which appears. However, philosophically and psychologically, the term needs further definition, explanation, and description. Phenomenology is a study of essences, such as the essence of imagination. It is also a study of transforming essences into reality, into existence.

DELIMITATION OF THE STUDY

Subject Delimitation

The scope of this research will be limited to the study of a branch of existential analysis represented by Adrian Van Kaam. It will also point out the counseling techniques, the schools of psychotherapy, and the philosophy of existentialism as the historical background of the ideas which ushered the existential counseling technique of Van Kaam.

Naturally, we are obliged to make a distinction between counseling in the school setting and counseling outside the school setting. In the former, counseling is broken down into personal, social, and vocational counseling. In the latter, we have marriage counseling, rehabilitation counseling, religious counseling, psychiatric therapy, and psychological therapy. Counseling whether practiced within or outside the school setting requires a specialized study, training, and experience. This thesis is confined to making an evaluation of a counseling technique which introduces an "authentic therapeutic attitude" underlying various kinds of counseling. The existential counseling of Van Kaam as a basic and fundamental orientation in promoting a client's search for his personal destiny can be applied to any form of counseling. The researcher whose interest is in college teaching and counseling has seen the relevance of existential counseling to college students. Hence, the limitation of the scope of the study of applying Van Kaam's technique to college students.

---

[13] Ibid., p. 359.

Importance of the Study

The suggested counseling technique based on Adrian Van Kaam's existential counseling when known has an essential implication to guidance and counseling and education which will redound to the formation of an authentic Filipino personality. The results of this study are valuable to the following groups of persons concerned with the formation of the total personality of college students:

1. Guidance counselors
2. Administrators
3. Teachers

Guidance Counselor. The guidance counselor who has gained an insight into existential counseling will have a deeper appreciation of the client's uniqueness and dignity as a human being. The emphasis on the personal encounter of counseling relationship will always be a constant challenge to the counselor to treat every client with awe and reverence because he is a person. Every encounter with the client is a "call" to the counselor to break from his narrow, self-centered interest in order to make possible for another human being to achieve self-actualization. Existential counseling will always challenge the counselor to be true to his work, to his commitment to be a man for others. It is this challenge to the counselor to be faithful to his vocation, to his profession so that he truly achieves his own self-actualization and his destiny.

Administrator. This research will also benefit the administrators in arousing their awareness of accepting the teachers, personnel, and students on the bases of their actual personal resources. On this facticity the administrator will always be motivated to set goals and objectives of the school within the limits of the possibilities of those under him. Furthermore, the existential counseling point of view that every man is potentially in crisis can make the administrator more human and understanding in his relationship with his subordinates. The administrator will be able to share with his teachers, personnel, and students the tragic sense of life. It will make the administrator realize that every person in his staff including himself will have his weak moments and will need the moral support of another human being in order to overcome the anxiety of having to live and to die with the courage to be.

The Teacher. Existential counseling can pave the way for the authoritarian Filipino teacher to be relaxed, democratic, and human. The awful and fearsome profile of a Filipino teacher who is rigid and tense continues to be a legacy to the present generation. Existential counseling can develop in the teacher the attitude to accept the anxiety and tension of what he is and what he ought to become. Too often the teachers or educators impose their values on the students without allowing the students to make their own choices and to determine their own values. In other words, in many educational institutions today, students are muzzled to do what they do not want to do. The implication of existential counseling to our teachers is the awareness to see possibilities in themselves as well as in their students. The teacher's role is to help the students accept themselves so that they can become what they want to become. Thus, existential counseling is a valuable tool in making the Filipino teachers accept that they too need counseling or psychotherapy more than their students.

METHODOLOGY

Techniques and Procedures Used

The method that will be used throughout the study is expository and critical. A brief description of the personality theories of Freud, Adler, and Frankl will be given to familiarize the readers with the schools of psychotherapy. The different theories of counseling techniques and their historical background will be analyzed. This will be followed by a discussion about existentialism. Then the researcher will present the main thrust of the thesis: Adrian Van Kaam's book *The Art of Existential Counseling*. Finally, the writer will go deeper into the relevance of Van Kaam's existential counseling technique as applied to college students, citing case studies to prove that the existential counseling technique is functional.

ORGANIZATION OF THE STUDY

This thesis is organized into four chapters. The beginning chapter includes the introduction, the problem, delimitation and scope of the study, definition of terms, and methodology: the techniques and procedures used and the organization of the study. The second chapter includes a review of related studies and literature, a discussion on the distinction between counseling and psychotherapy, the three schools of psychotherapy: Freudian psychoanalysis, Adlerian individual psychology and Franklian logotherapy, presentation of the three counseling techniques: directive, non-directive, and the eclectic, and presents the philosophy of existentialism and its implications to counseling. The third chapter deals with Van Kaam's idea of the existential counseling technique, the features of other existential philosophy, and answers the question of the relevance of Van Kaam's existential counseling technique in counseling college students. The last chapter gives the summary, conclusion, and recommendations of the study. Possible research problems in relation to the present study are also suggested in this chapter.

CHAPER II

REVIEW OF LITERATURE

Related studies are theses and dissertations and independent researches or perhaps sponsored researches which undergo steps in problem solving.

Related literature are broader, includes formal scientific papers, textbooks and reference books, articles in magazines and newspapers, speeches, bulletins, memoranda, and lectures delivered.

The two works of Juan Lamela[14] on existentialism are analytical studies of the existentialist position. The first work is a critical evaluation of Karl Jaspers, Idea of God. It is somewhat related to the present study because Van Kaam borrows ontological truths from Philosophy to build his hypothetical constructs of existential counseling. Lamela's work, however, is limited to philosophical analysis, whereas the present study goes into the specific actual and concrete unveiling of man's relationship with God on Reality.

The finding of Lamela's research on Jasper is that the concept of God is real and not just a fiction of the imagination. God as a being is beyond thinking, is an object, and cannot be grasped in rational terms. Another finding of Lamela is that Jasper's idea of God establishes the relationship between religion and philosophy. The two go together to make the whole adventure of man exciting. Without religion, man's philosophizing will lose the dynamics center.

---

[14] Juan Lamela, The Idea of God in Karl Jaspers Philosophy (Unpublished Master's Thesis, University of San Carlos, Cebu City, March, 1965), pp. 72-74.

The second work of Lamela[15] has the same limitation as the first. This is understandable because Lamela is primarily an existentialist philosopher and philosopher of education. He never intended his first two works to be integrated into the art and practice of counseling and psychotherapy.

The conclusion of Lamela on Ortega y Gassett's "Idea of a University" is that the university should serve not only its own academic community but also the larger community or the whole of reality. In other words, the involvement and commitment of the university is the whole of life. It must always be ready to guide the scientific, cultural, and professional life of the times. By being true to its commitment, the university will be fulfilling its mission and destiny as a spiritual power to the society.

The work of Johnson[16] is an analytical study that makes use of the existentialist approach to personality. Johnson's research is an analysis of the problems of a foreign missionary in his dealings with the Filipino personality. His work and the writer's study are similar in its affirmation of the uniqueness of the person, his culture, and his society. The limitation of Johnson's study is that its emphasis is confined to the psychosocial approach of the structure of the Filipino personality as applied to pastoral counseling. The writer's study is concerned in formulating a comprehensive-theoretical framework within the psychotherapeutic relationship between counselor and counselee, it confines its investigations into the structure of man's existence and how the counselor can help a disturbed person grow in freedom and responsibility.

The conclusion of Johnson is that the Filipino personality characteristics affect the counseling processes, particularly in the area of pastoral counseling. The authoritarianism, *hiya*, *pakikisama, amor propio,* and others are some of the traits of the Filipino personality which foreign missionaries encountered and against which they had difficulties on account of their different frame of reference.

---

15 Juan Lamela, Jose Ortega y Gasset, Idea of the University and Its Relevance to the Present Status of Higher Education in the Philippines (Unpublished Master's Thesis, University of San Carlos, Cebu City, March, 1968), pp. 158-160.

16 James L. Johnson, Pastoral Counseling in the Philippines (Unpublished Master's Thesis, University of San Carlos, Cebu City, March, 1965), pp. 146-160.

The research of Buenaventura[17] is a critical exposition of modern man's estrangement from his fellowmen and from his God. Her study is related to the writer's study under the aspect of man's freedom and responsibility. Buenaventura's research is more concerned with the literary expression of man's loneliness and helplessness in a world filled with doubt and uncertainty.

The finding of Buenaventura's research on Graham Greene's work is the predominance of suffering and evil. The characters of Greene's novels are men and women tormented by guilt, fear, and frustrations of having to live and to suffer. The interplay of good and evil makes man conscious of the struggle within himself to achieve his self-actualization. Only when man has learned to accept his suffering and find meaning in his suffering can he be conscious of a God.

Cimafranca's[18] work is a critical analysis of modern philosophies on ethics with emphasis on existentialism. It treats the subject matter in an abstract and general framework, citing the historical background of modern day situation ethics philosophy. Cimafranca's research is related and relevant to the present study especially its emphasis on the history of ideas which has shaped the modern temper. The difference with this writer's research is its emphasis to go beyond history—its analysis and emphasis is in man's existence and his reality.

The finding of Cimafranca's research is that situation ethics contradicts natural law. His reasoning is that since situation ethics is an offshoot of existentialism and existentialism is based on personal experience, it follows that situation ethics distorts reality. Situation ethics, therefore, must be rejected for its acceptance will lead to a breakdown of Judeo-Christian tradition.

Cavada's[19] research is a critical analysis of man's relationship with his fellowmen. The present study has a common ground with Cavada's emphasis

---

17 Amparo Buenaventura, Religious Ideas in the Novels of Graham Greene (Unpublished Master's Thesis, University of San Carlos, Cebu City, March, 1965), pp. 123-127.

18 Eliseo Cimafranca, The Metaphysical Background of Situational (Unpublished Master's Thesis, University of San Carlos, Cebu City, October, 1969)

19 Jose Noel Cavada, The Problem of Alienation in the Philosophy of Labor from the Personalist Standpoint (Unpublished Master's Thesis, University of San Carlos, Cebu City, March, 1973), pp. 89-94.

on man's dignity and his worth as a person. Whereas the present writer is concerned with the dynamic of man's therapeutic relationships, Cavada's work is confined to man's feeling of alienation in his work.

The conclusion of the study of Cavada is that the average worker in the modern world spends most of his time in the factory and his personality is greatly affected by this interaction. It is then the obligation of industrial and economic planners to make the working conditions of the average man more human by being more responsive to man's higher needs. Such reorientation of the direction of progress must take man as the center of interest by creating a climate responsive to his needs and interests as a human being.

The conclusion of Kierkegaard[20] is that man's inward experience or subjectivity is the measure of truth. Through personal experience, man as a being in the world can decide the truth of his existence.

Nietzche's[21] conclusion is that philosophy based on personal experience should lead us to the affirmation that the human existence is the striving to be a superman. The superman is the embodiment of all the noble virtues in man which make him transcend the limitations of his culture and society.

Husserl's[22] assertion is that man discovers the meaning of existence by taking hold of the given and personal experience. Although Husserl calls his approach phenomenological, he has influenced existentialism in his emphasis on man as "being there" who can perceive the "being-for-me" of others.

Heidegger's[23] conclusion is that man is the only creature who can ask about his being a man. As a man, he is capable of consciousness and reflection whether or not his existence is authentic or inauthentic.

Sartre's[24] conclusion is that man is a being who exists and who must create his essence. Man determines who he is and what he wants to become.

---

20 Soren Kierkegaard, as quoted by Will Herberg, ed. *Four Existentialist Theologians* (New York: Doubleday and Company, Inc., 1959), pp. 1-9.

21 Frederick W. Nietzsche, "The Will to Power in Nature," *Six Existentialist Thinkers* (N.J. Blackham, New York: Harper and Row, 1959), pp. 115-116.

22 J. Donald Butler, *Four Philosophies* (New York: Harper and Row, 1957), pp. 440-441.

23 M. Heidegger as quoted by Brock, "An Account of Time and Being," *Six Existentialist Thinkers*, N.J. Blackham (ed.) New York: Harper & Row, 1959), pp. 240-292.

24 Jean-Paul Sartre, *Existentialism and Human Emotions* (New York: The Wisdom Library, 1951), p. 10.

May's[25] conclusion is that man is in the world and his being is always in the process of emerging or becoming. In other words, man is potentially in crisis at any given moment in his life. This potentiality in man to be in crisis is a challenge for man to actualize his being a man.

The emphasis of Kierkegaard, Nietzsche, Husserl, and Sartre is on philosophy. May, however, has an active interest in counseling and psychotherapy and his approach is based on Heidegger's philosophy. The writer's research on the other hand, is about Van Kaam's existential counseling, a branch of existential analysis, a school of psychology which propagates existentialism and its implications to counseling and psychotherapy.

Inquiry into other materials available allows us to conclude that nobody has written on Adrian Van Kaam's Existential Counseling and its application to college students. Hence, this treatise is the first so far to be written.

COUNSELING AND PSYCHOTHERAPY

In recent years, one of the most hotly debated issues is the distinction between counseling and psychotherapy. Most authors do not draw the line but have simply accepted and used the two terms synonymously. Part of the reason is the confusion within the ranks of counselors and psychotherapists respectively as to their specific roles, functions, and goals. Counselors as well as psychotherapists are of various shapes and colors. To the average person, counselors operate in the school setting and they are called school counselors, guidance counselors, and counseling psychologists. Their qualifications range from a few units earned in graduate work to highly holders of MA and PHD degrees in guidance and counseling. Psychologists are those who hold an MA or PhD in psychology and are employed in the military, government, industries, hospitals, social agencies, or are simply engaged in private practice as clinicians. Their methodologies and procedures in dealing with clients differ depending upon their theoretical allegiance. Whatever differences in approaches they may use in helping a client solve his problem there is one limitation they all share in common. Psychologists cannot prescribe medicine, drugs, or any form of tranquilizers for the client. The psychiatrist on the other hand is one who holds an MD degree with a background in psychology. Only he, the medical practitioner, can

---

[25] Rollo, May, *Existential Psychology* (New York: Random House, Inc., 1961), p. 16.

administer drugs, give injections, or use chemotherapy on the client. In the understanding of most people, psychologists and counselors in schools practice counseling while the psychologists outside of the school setting are entrusted with clients facing serious problems, deep-seated emotional problems such as complexes, disturbances, neurosis, and even psychosis. It is presupposed that in the schools there are very few serious problems and if there are any, these are or should be referred to the experts, the PhDs in psychology who will assist the client in tracing the causes of the disturbance in the unconscious. If the problem of the client is so serious that there is a personality disintegration, then the client will have to be hospitalized under the care of a psychiatrist. Thus, superficially, counselors in schools are engaged in counseling—handling problems of normal people in the realm of the vocational, personal, and social levels of existence. The psychologists and psychiatrists deal with persons whose problems are considered serious because their behavioral patterns have degrees of deviation from the behavior of a normal, well adjusted person in society to a person who has escaped from reality. It is then easy to discern why the man on the street assumes that the role of the psychologist and the psychiatrist is that of practicing psychotherapy, the former using the technique of verbalization in making the patient talk about his past and explore his unconscious, the latter using both verbalization and drugs.

Looking objectively on the professional status of the counselor in school, the psychologist or the clinician, and the psychiatrist, does not give us an insight as to what is counseling and what is psychotherapy, where one begins and where the other ends, and vice-versa.

There are those who maintain that counseling deals with normal individuals while psychotherapy deals with the abnormal. Others will say that counseling operates on the conscious level or the cognitive and rational faculties while psychotherapy handles the region of the dark unconscious. Some consider counseling as an approach to mild problems whereas psychotherapy is for deep and serious problems of the personality.

Mowrer,[26] for example, holds the point of view that counseling relationship is giving assistance "to persons suffering from fully conscious conflicts, which are accompanied by so called normal anxiety."

---

[26] Hobart Mowrer, "Anxiety Theory as a Basis for Distinguishing Between Counseling and Psychotherapy," in Ralph F. Berdie (ed.) *Concepts of Programs of Counseling* (Minneapolis: University of Minnesota Press, 1951), p. 23.

In Tyler's[27] therapeutic framework, psychotherapy involves personality change, whereas counseling is to help the individual make use of inner resources to face life.

Boden's[28] system holds that psychotherapy tends to explore the emotional side of man rather than his intellectual faculty, which is the emphasis of counseling.

There are those who hold a medical degree and think that the practice of psychotherapy is their exclusive domain while those who are not MDs practice counseling. This point of view is not tenable for PhDs in psychology who are not licensed MDs and who are doing the same work as their medical colleagues, except prescribe medicine. The problem is further made complicated by the fact that within the ranks of medical practitioners there is a dogmatic belief that only psychoanalysis can be considered valid psychotherapy. To this group belong the followers of Fromme-Reichman. This approach to therapy based on one school of psychotherapy will certainly invite opposition from psychotherapies that are not psychoanalysis, both the MD and non-MD who belong to the camps of Jung, Adler, Frankl, Rogers, Van Kaam and Tillich. Historically, Freud, the father of psychoanalysis, has stressed that one need not be a holder of a medical degree to be a successful therapist. Why the medical colleagues of Freud see the necessity of a medical background to be able to solve problems that are psychological in nature still remains to be one of the unresolved issues in our times.

The various differentiations between psychotherapy and counseling such as unconscious and conscious, serious and mild cases, psychotic and neurotic, emotional and intellectual, may exist on the theoretical order. Moreover, the school counselor in his daily experience will have a hard time distinguishing between the two. It does not matter whether he is dealing with children or with adults. Anyone familiar with the job of a counselor knows the varied relationships that he initiates with the students. In some children he explores their emotions and feelings; others he says a word or two to inspire them to relate their past background and conditioning; still with others he will concentrate on their present problem and guide them to learn to be more effective students in the future. There are also some students whose problems

---

27 Leona E. Tyler, *The Work of the Counselor* (New York: Appleton-Century Crofts, 1961), p. 12.

28 Edward S. Boden, *Psychological Counseling* (New York: Appleton-Century Crofts, 1955), p. 15.

are apparently on the cognitive level but whose underlying causes stem from unconscious pressures of parents, students, and other children. In all these relationships with the students, the counselor is swamped by materials coming from both the conscious and the unconscious and thus it becomes difficult to draw the line on whether he is doing counseling or psychotherapy. Of course, one thing is definite in the work of a counselor and that is, he seldom meets a student who is not in contact with reality, and they are the psychotics; however, if he happens to be very sensitive, he is aware of the opportunity of meeting students who would like to escape from reality and these are neurotics. In this case, the distinction is quite clear. Nevertheless, the work of the counselor involves coming in contact with different persons under stress and to establish the boundary between the subconscious and the conscious levels would be like attempting to determine whether a swimmer is submerged underwater or out of the water, when in fact he is both. The only way a school counselor and administrator can get out of the dilemma is to really be effective in his work and not be bothered about semantics. If the term "psychotherapy" is frightening and threatening to him, then he may go on with his work and call his function "counseling."

THE SCHOOLS OF PSYCHOTHERAPY

In this chapter the three schools of psychotherapy will be discussed, namely: The Freudian Psychoanalysis, the Adlerian Will to Power, and the Franklian Logotherapy. There are of course many other schools of psychotherapy with their own theoretical framework just as there are many techniques of counseling and psychotherapy. The writer cannot give an exhaustive treatment of the other psychotherapies, for that would no longer fall within the scope of the thesis. It is sufficient that the ideas of the founders of the different leading psychotherapies be presented.

Sigmund Freud's Pleasure-Principle

The point of departure in the understanding of Freudian psychoanalysis is in the libido theory of life-energy.[29] The libido is the psychic energy which

---

[29] J. Maritain, *Scholasticism and Politics* (New York: Doubleday and Company, Inc., 1960), pp. 153-155.

gives the human organism its needs, drives, urges, instincts, and so forth. The libido may take two different courses of direction: one towards *eros* or life instinct which includes the primary drives of thirst, hunger, and sex; the other is *thanatos* or the death instinct, which includes every urge in man that motivates him to self-destruction. The existence of a human organism is determined by this vital force which has both positive and negative effects on the development of a personality. It all depends upon how this life instinct is properly distributed to every individual. The personality construct of Freud is based on the economic distribution of the libido.

According to Freud, human nature is composed of *id*, *ego,* and *superego.*[30] Each is a structure within a total personality, each is a unity which interacts with other structures. The behavior of an individual is the result of the interaction of the *id*, *ego*, and the *superego.*

The constitutive structure of the id lies in the physical aspect of the human organism and its inherited traits and characteristics, instincts, and tendencies. The id is called the pleasure-principle because its thrust is towards achievement of pleasure and avoidance of pain. It is the meeting place of the physical and the psychological. The transformation of the physical and psychic energy becomes the source of power for the ego and the superego.

The ego, on the other hand, is the reality principle. It is dependent on the id for the source of psychic energy and owes its development to the instinctual drives. Although the ego cooperates with the id and satisfies the instincts' craving for pleasure, its function is to control intelligence and perception. It is the ego that serves as the guide for the individual in dealing and coming to some forms of adjustment within his environment.

The third and last portion of the personality is the superego. Its function is to come in contact with the mores, customs, and traditions of society. The internalization of the morality in a given society makes the individual curb his aggressive and sexual impulses that have their origin from the id. The superego determines the higher values and goals different from the realistic ones adopted by the ego.[31]

This, in a nutshell, is the closed system of the dynamic operation and interaction of the id, the ego, and the superego. This is the key to our understanding of the economic distribution of the libido as well as our

---

[30] Allan W. Watts, *Psychotherapy East and West* (New York: Mentor-Omega Book, 1962), pp. 277-283.

[31] Karl Stern, *The Third Revolution* (New York: Image Books, 1961), pp. 74-76.

insight into the Freudian personality construct. In order to have a full grasp of the libido theory and Freud's view of man and his personality, we need to explain the psychoanalytical theory of infantile sexuality.

In Freud's schemata, there are five phases or stages which every man passes before he attains the full awareness and self-realization as a normal human being. These five stages are the following: the oral stage, the anal stage, the phallic stage, the latent stage, and the genital stage. The first three stages occur during the first six years of an individual's life and all neurosis is traceable to what happens during this period. The oral stage is the infant's experience of pleasure as his mouth comes in contact with objects. Communication with the environment takes place in the mouth. When the need for satisfaction of the infant's need for milk, which is the symbol of the warmth, care, and love of a mother, is wanting, then there arises the problem of fixation. Fixation means that a certain sexual energy or libido continues to be attached to any one of the five stages. Thus, a child may reach the latent stage and still be fixated in the oral stage if he continues, for example, the habit of thumbsucking. Among the adults, smoking and drinking are some practices which many psychoanalysts have interpreted as outcomes of the fixation in the oral stage.

The anal stage is characterized by the infant's preoccupation with the pleasure that he derives from his anus. There is a pleasant sensation in holding and withholding his bowel movement. There is self-centered curiosity in what takes place before and after defecation. This is the reason why he takes a great deal of interest in playing with his feces. Fixations which have their origin in the anal stage are certain forms of constipation.

The phallic stage is the child's shift of interest to his reproductive organ. This period, in which attention is attracted to other objects, is known as "object libido." This development is in contrast to the oral and anal stages in which the child seizes his own body as its "ego-libido." In the phallic stage, the child develops a bond with either the mother or father. According to this theory, the boy falls in love with the mother while the girl with the father; the mother and the father become the respective objects of the libido. For the boy, this phenomenon is called the Oedipus Complex while for the girl it is known as the Electra Complex. During this period, the boy looks at his father as his rival in his love for his mother, his feeling for his father is ambivalent. On one hand, he is jealous of the love relationship between his father and mother. Later on, the complex is dissolved and desexualized as the boy realizes the impossibility of attaining his love-object. Furthermore, there is the fear of castration and the whole Oedipus Complex collapses.

The boy identifies with the father (identification), the girl with the mother. At this point the latent period begins. The latent period takes place from the sixth to the ninth years. During these years the child is not preoccupied with sexual curiosity and the mental phenomenon that occurs during this period is often referred to as "infantile amnesia."

The fourth and last stage is the genital period. This is the beginning of adult sexuality in which man takes an active interest in the opposite sex. Freud's originality lies in the fact that he looks at sexuality not only from the age of puberty but also from infancy. Before Freud, no one dared to think that the sexual development of man is a build up of psychic energy from the time we are formed to the time we die and that the first movement is from infancy, while the second movement is from the age of puberty.

Another original contribution of Freud's psychology and which occupies a central position in his theory of the personality is the theory of the unconscious. The unconscious is the realm in which conflicting tendencies in the conscious mind (usually sexual in nature) are repressed and submerged to live a separate existence. The unconscious is different from the pre-conscious in the sense that the latter are forgotten memories, events, and happenings which can easily be recalled by the conscious mind. The unconscious on the other hand are former objects of tendency that is denied existence in the conscious mind and becomes a psychic content apart from the conscious.

Other theories of Freud such as suppression, regression, rationalization, projection, reaction formation, compensation, displacement, and others are built around the theory of the unconscious in relation to libido, id, ego, and superego and the genetic theory.

Sigmund Freud's school of psychotherapy looks at man as a creature motivated in human activity based on the pleasure-principle. Man's psychic apparatus is guided by life energy or libido distributed into the forces of the id, ego, and the superego. Furthermore, Freud shows how man reaches his personality fulfillment through the different stages starting from infancy to the genital period. Finally, the unconscious must never be omitted for it is important in the understanding of the interaction of the id, ego, and superego, the genetic theory and the different forms of defense mechanisms.

Alfred Adler's Will to Power

Alfred Adler was at one time a collaborator of Freud. Like Carl Jung of Zurich, Adler was not the kind of man that can be led by the nose; his independent mind led him to disagree with Freud on the theory of sexuality. This dissatisfaction with the pleasure-principle resulted in the formal break of the two Vienna-based psychiatrists in 1902, the same year in which Adler was invited by Freud to join the psychoanalytical circle.

The new school of psychotherapy of Adler is known as Individual Psychology. It goes by that name because the founder and leader of this school of thought lays emphasis on the uniqueness of the individual human being as an indivisible unity; there are no two individuals who are alike; each has a striving towards a goal in which there can be no duplication.

This striving in man towards a goal is borne out of a need for perfection and is called the will to power. Man feels insecure, inadequate, and imperfect and as a consequence he is motivated by a vital force to rise above his limitations. For Adler this is the rationale for all our interest and other involvement in human activity. We act and get involved in society because we want to excel.

The discovery of the Will to Power is not new.[32] It was mentioned by other thinkers, particularly Nietzsche. What is original in Adler lies in the way he develops the theory into personality construct beginning in childhood.

The child's world is full of wants, longings, and needs. Very early in life he learns how helpless he is in getting everything he wants. Whereas the adults do not have difficulty in obtaining their objects and satisfying their desires, the child is often thwarted in pursuing his own needs. The pressures of the adults to make him behave and conform to their ways are brought home to him in his tender years. He becomes frustrated and gradually accepts the demands of the adults to make him conform to their wishes. This early experience of submission to a power external to him develops the inferiority feeling towards those who are superior to him. He feels the superiority of adults because they can threaten, coerce, and force him to follow their bidding. Thus, in his play the child plays the role of a soldier, driver, doctor, father, mother, etc. This is manifestation of the striving for perfection or inferiority feelings. The acting out of his fantasy is actually a need to overcome his inferiority in the midst of superior adults; it is his self-transcendence from the feeling of being dwarfed by the limitations of his environment and to arrive at his goal of becoming what he should be as

---

[32] Joseph Nuttin, *Psychoanalysis and Personality* (New York: Mentor-Omega Book, 1962), pp. 277-283.

a superior being. This is the level of awareness in the dynamic movement in the psychic life.[33]

The second movement in the psychic life of the individual is towards the community life. Man is not just a creature destined to live for oneself, but he is also a being whose existence is rooted in the desire to be a man for others. Man's struggle at self-integration, autonomy, and independence of existence is one aspect of his tendencies embedded in the biological necessity of self-preservation. Although the individual must take care of himself and promote his good, man has another tendency to go beyond himself, towards the common good, towards the communion of feelings with his fellowmen. The will to power gives way to the will to community. Adler maintains that altruism, all civic-mindedness, and other expressions of social consciousness and responsibility can be attributed to the individual's striving to break away from the bondage of egocentrism on the level of the will to power.

In the early stages of a child's development, the community feeling is dim. Although it is present in his yearnings, the child's world is basically centered on his ego and how his demands can be met. The striving of a child is to get everything and it is understandable because of his dependence on and parasitic existence of those around him. He cannot give because he has nothing to give, but the potential to share is imminent in him.

The will to community is the goal towards which the child has to evolve. Towards this objective, it is necessary that the child begins with self-assertion or will to power, for it is the foundation of a personality. From the feeling of elation and confidence in his power, the child must learn to go out from his shell of egocentricity towards a sense of community. This is a crucial test and a painful experience as one undertakes the responsibility to achieve his self-realization through interaction with his fellowmen. How to give oneself, how to be a man for others, is very difficult for a man who has not taken his first step. To make the decision and accept one's responsibility to others takes a lot of courage. For Adler those who lack the self-confidence and courage to take the first step from the egocentric world to the world of sharing in community life run the risk of neurosis. It is the root cause of all complexes and disturbances in the lives of individuals.

As a personality theorist, Adler's emphasis is on the "creative self" of the individual as the "first cause" of behavior. He did not share Freud's

---

[33] Jane Walters, *Techniques of Counseling* (New York: McGraw-Hill Book Company, 1964), pp. 389-390.

view that man is determined by developmental stages and the Oedipus Complex. Although Adler agrees with Freud that the first six years of life is crucial in the formation of the personality, the direction of his thought leans heavily on social interest. Since social interest or the will to community is for Adler the crowning glory of the personality, he rejects a deterministic conception of man. He does not look for the "why" of man's behavior in hereditary factors, family circumstance, and environment. Adler looks at the individual and his specific task and situation. He accepts the individual as such, as he is in his totality as he confronts the world, Adler maintains that his school of psychotherapy can detect the plan, the goal, and the lifestyle of the individual.

It is "creative self" that determines the lifestyle of the individual. Man's thrust should be to look for experiences that will intensify his goal or objective in life. This view of finality makes man a creator of his values as well as the values of society. It transforms man into a being of many possibilities who has to realize his unique self as an individual with a will to power and as a social being with a will to community.

Victor Frankl's Logotherapy

Victor Frankl is one of the survivors of the Nazi concentration camp at Auschwitz. His courage and determination to maintain his integrity and decency in the midst of human degradation tell us of man's ability to rise above the limitation of environment, situations, and circumstances. Man need not be determined nor conditioned by outward restrictions for man is not a robot or machine. No matter what circumstances man will be thrown into, he has the innate resources to survive and endure the hardships. The study of Frankl and how he survived the ordeal in Auschwitz and other Nazi camps is a deeply moving story. It tells us that incredible suffering and human degradation can be overcome if we know the "why" of our existence. As long as man knows the "why," he can cope with any situation or reality; the "how" necessarily follows.[34]

The personal experience of Frankl as a prisoner during World War II is the background as well as the foundation of Logotherapy. *Logos* means meaning or spirit. As a system of psychotherapy, Logotherapy is concerned with man's existence in the world and his search for meaning. Unlike Freud

---

[34] Frankl, *op. cit.*, pp. 156-163.

who looks at man as a being motivated by the will to pleasure and Adler's will to power, Frankl sees man possessing a will to meaning. This will to meaning is all that man has as he makes a leap to existence and comes face to face with the problem of how to exist in the human way. There is no abstract and universal prescription of the meaning of life. Each man must search and discover his own meaning in a specific task, vocation, project, or mission. There can be no duplication of this vocation or task and only the individual himself can determine his own goal and fulfill it. This is what gives man his cause, ideals, and values. This deeply-rooted drive in him, beyond the level of urges and instincts, makes men truly live and die as a human being.

The failure of a human being to achieve his authenticity is the consequence of his failure to discover a meaningful value. In the course of every man's life, the individual aspires toward a certain degree of meaningful existence and when such aspiration is blocked or thwarted, man is frustrated. The existential analyst calls it the "existential frustration." Although Frankl also uses the term existential frustration, he gives it a specific and scientific term known as "noogenic neurosis." "*Noos*" is etymologically derived from the Greek which means mind. In Frankl's schemata, neurosis is a disturbance which has its root cause in the mind and has a spiritual dimension because it involves conflict of values. Spiritual dimension in Logotherapy does not necessarily mean religious value but man's projected goal of existence and his courage to actualize his meaning.[35]

As a theorist of personality, Frankl introduces another term which he calls "noodynamics"—the theory that man needs a certain amount of conflict and tension to maintain an inner equilibrium. As opposite to homeostasis, the tensionless state, noodynamics encourages the striving and struggling in man's nature as prerequisite for mental health. In a state of tension, man is able to reflect on what he has accomplished and what more can be accomplished; he moves from what he has been to what he is and what he can become. Noodynamics therefore orientates man to detect his values and ideals. The lack of direction and goal in life is what causes the "existential vacuum" in the life of modern man. It is the characteristic of modern man's life to despair of life. Life is for the majority sterile, flat, and empty. The meaninglessness of life manifests itself under many forms of disguises, such as will to pleasure, will to power, will to money, etc. These are manifestations of man's attempt to escape his awareness of the life task which only he can fulfill. The more

---

[35] Victor Frankl, *The Doctor of the Soul* (New York: Alfred A. Kroft, 1955), p. 12.

he tries to distract his attention from his true vocation, the more he is caught in the vicious circle of his "noogenic neurosis." The salvation of man from boredom, despair, and suicide is for man to search for meaning in his life.

The meaning of one's life can only be answered by the particular individual, concrete man as he confronts the challenge of life to find his own specific life task; man is always addressed by life to which he must give his responses. Man's dialogue with life must always be to be true and responsible to life. The meaning of existence can be actualized or transformed into reality in three ways: performing some work such as teaching, writing, serving those in need, and so forth; experiencing a value like committing oneself to a cause or living and dying for an ideal; and by suffering. To be able to live and accept suffering bravely can be a source of joy. It is to take up an attitude in which suffering has a new meaning because one has discovered a spiritual dimension in it. Logotherapy as a psychotherapy awakens us to the spiritual realities of human existence. Modern man's helplessness in the modern world lies in his failure to confront the meaning of existence as it is given to every man in a concrete life task.

The thrust of Logotherapy is the future of man and his world and only man can fulfill his own meaning and actualize his values.

THE THREE COUNSELING TECHNIQUES

I. THE DIRECTIVE TECHNIQUE

There are several approaches or techniques in counseling. Since there are three most widely known and used techniques of counseling, the writer will concentrate on these three, namely: the directive, the nondirective, and the eclectic.

The directive technique of counseling has always been associated with traditional psychiatry. In the history of psychiatry, the therapist has always assumed the role of directing the thinking, the emotional life, and the behavior of the patient. According to Appel[36], this was a necessary condition for a successful therapy because of the psychological and emotional immaturity of

---

[36] K. E. Appel as quoted by McKinney, "Directive Counseling," *An Introduction to Clinical Psychology*, Pennington and Berg eds. (New York: Donald Press, Co., 1948), p. 443.

the patient who must be dependent on the psychiatrist or psychotherapist. Following Appel's line of thinking, it is easy to discern that the psychotherapeutic practices evolve from psychiatric practice and personnel guidance with the psychologist's role to direct clients in the resolutions of their conflicts.

Under the directive method, counseling is seen and objectively looked at as a direction, as giving of assistance in effectively promoting the process of adjustment and involves guidance function rather than control or dominance. Thus, therapeutic cure hinges on the personality of the counselor, training, reputation, methods, and resources. On the other side of the counseling relationship, so much depends on the maturity, intelligence, and stability of the client to accept direction.[37]

The goal of directive therapy is self-understanding, self-acceptance, and self-control. The counselor who uses this technique creates the condition and the situation in which he can satisfy the client's need to understand himself by exploring his motives and tentatively achieving an integration on a stable and mature level. This the counselor does by giving the client minimal responsibility he can assure to understand himself. The counselor may bring out in the open his explanations of the client's anxieties, frustrations, complexes, and adjustment mechanisms. However, the client must be spared from the overwhelming impact of the truth about himself. It is necessary and imperative that the client need not go into details and the implications of his revelation to the counselor be interpreted for him in small doses.

The client must be given the opportunity to verbalize his anxiety, probe into his unconscious, and make his own discoveries—no matter how superficial they may appear to the counselor. The counselor should respect the pace and rhythm of the client's discovery of himself in his own manner. The role of the counselor is to inspire the counselee to make his own initiative, not force or coerce him to face prematurely some aspects of his personality associated with anxiety.

When the counseling interview is not moving towards successful therapy, the counselor may subtly raise questions. If the client encounters obstacles to go on or if the counseling relationship has reached an impasse, the counselor may interrogate, interpret, suggest, or bring out similar cases to bring back the client to a level of awareness and stimulation. In his moment

---

[37] F.C. Thorne, "Directive Psychotherapy: III-The Psychology of Simple Maladjustment," *Modern Methods of Counseling*, Arthur H. Grayfield, ed. (New York: Appleton-Century-Crofts, Inc., 1950) pp. 158-160.

of boredom, discouragement, or just plain thinking in circles, the counselee must be handled with utmost care so as not to lose the rapport.[38]

Williamson[39] has enumerated six steps involved in directive counseling: analysis, synthesis, diagnosis, prognosis, counseling, and follow-up.

Analysis is the gathering of information and other pertinent data about the student; synthesis, the putting together of all the traits and characteristics of a student's personality; diagnosis, the formulation of tentative conclusions about the background of a student's problems. Counseling is being with and for the student in his attempt to remove blocks and obstacles to know himself; and follow-up is determining the success and failure of procedures used in solving the student's problems and helping students either to meet new problems or the recurrence of old ones. What should be remembered always is that the heart of directive counseling is in the counseling relationship itself. It is the care, attention, and warmth that the counselor gives to the counselee that is the crux of directive counseling therapy. All other information about the student will become meaningless without the man to man relationship in the counseling atmosphere.

Since directive counseling involves guidance functions it cannot extricate itself from the imposition of values. The counselor, being also an educator, has the duty to influence the students to form desirable and constructive values that promote the best interest of society. The counselor in his interaction and behavior with the students in the nature of his work is in the best position to identify the wholesome and meaningful lifestyles. He can assist the students to come to terms with alternative value systems, leaving the area of free decision an option open to the students.[40]

Directive counseling as a product of traditional psychiatry does not remove the freedom, the self-direction, and permissive atmosphere for the client. It implements its goals not by preaching, admonishing, ordering, or coercing the student to follow a certain pattern of behavior. It does give information, diagnosis, and value orientation to the student to enhance his decision for self-direction.

---

[38] Fred McKinney, "Directive Counseling," *An Introduction to Clinical Psychology*, Pennington and Berg, eds. (New York: Ronald Press Co., 1948), p. 443.

[39] E.G. Williamson, "Three Approaches to Counseling Interview," *Techniques of Counseling*, Warters, ed. (New York: McGraw-Hill Book Company, 1964), p. 435.

[40] *Ibid.*, pp. 437-438.

II. THE NON-DIRECTIVE

The development of the non-directive technique of counseling is said to have its origins in the writings of Otto Rank[41] and Jessie Taft. Otto Rank, one of the brilliant pupils of Sigmund Freud, postulated the theory that psychotherapeutic relationship is a conflict situation of two persons. In such a relationship the patient should be given the chance to dominate the therapist. This is because every individual needs to reenact and re-experience the birth trauma whose separation from the mother causes emotional pain in every newborn child. According to Rank's theory, every life experience is a duplication and repetition of the birth trauma. Lack of adjustment to the environment is therefore a lack of adjustment to the separation and isolation of the child from the mother. This unresolved separation of the child to his mother is Rank's explanation of the cause of neurosis. In the therapeutic relationship the disturbed individual is made to re-experience and readjust to the separation represented by the psychotherapist. The healing process takes place in the vicarious experiencing of the birth trauma and even the ending of the treatment is symbolic of the separation and the beginning of the liberation from one's complexes or neurosis.

Jessie Taft[42] on the other hand placed a great deal of emphasis on the therapeutic relationship between two persons. He was more concerned with the relationship rather than the intellectual decisions and explanations which take place during the interview. Furthermore, the thrust of Taft's ideas is to establish a framework for a therapeutic encounter that is free, open, and permissive for the client to relate and express what he felt.

This view became very popular in the United States from 1930s to the 1940s. It was elaborated by John Levy's relationship therapy. David Levy's attitude therapy and Frederick Allen's approach therapy with children are among the offshoots of the movement started by Rank and Taft.[43] Carl Rogers, who was influenced by this new trend in counseling and

---

[41] Will O. Rank, *Therapy: Truth and Reality* (New York: Kraft, 1945), pp. 32-38.

[42] J.J. Taft, *The Dynamics of Therapy in a Controlled Relationship* (New York: MacMillan, 1933), p. 73.

[43] William J. Snyder, "Client-Centered Therapy," *An Introduction to Clinical Psychology*, Pennington and Berg, eds. (New York: Ronald Press, Co., 1948), p. 466.

psychotherapy, published his book on the non-directive approach in 1940.[44] As years passed, Rogers was able to establish himself with distinction as leader of the non-directive movement. Today the movement has gained momentum among American psychiatrists, educators, and counselors and is identified as client-centered—the term coined by Karl Rogers himself.

The non-directive technique of counseling is characterized by warm, understanding, relaxing and objective therapeutic relationship in which the client can discuss personal matters in an atmosphere of openness and spontaneity.[45] The counselor's acceptance of the client is the core of the therapeutic cure and this takes place in an accepting environment. Counselor-client relationship is reserved and objective yet cheerful, without the superficiality and easy optimism which is characteristic of Dale Carnegie and Billy Graham's styles of meeting people. The counselors are persons who are on a stable and mature level of emotional life, full of warmth and care and objectivity. The personality, training, and experience of the counselor have a tremendous influence in making the client ventilate his emotions.

The underlying principle of the non-directive method of counseling is a fusion of negative and positive approaches to the personality. It is negative in a sense that it avoids giving information, asking of questions, offering, and persuasion. It is positive because it clarifies and recognizes the client's feelings, it creates a situation of simple acceptance of the client's statements, and it explains the structure (structuring of the counselor-and-client relationship) of their respective roles to work together in order to solve the problem.[46]

When the client meets for the first time the counselor who is client-centered, he is at once reassured by the latter's recognition of his (client's) feelings. The counselor accepts the negative and positive feelings of the client in an environment in which he is free from inhibition. The client's experience of freedom makes him feel relaxed and warm. It reconditions him to the pleasant thought that he is understood by another human being. He also gains at the same time the insight that the freedom in the therapeutic encounter uncovers his freedom to work out his own problems in his own

---

[44] C.R. Rogers, *Counseling and Psychology* (Boston: Houghton Mifflin, 1942), pp. 61-67.

[45] Carl Rogers and Rosalind Dymond (eds.) *Psychotherapy and Personality Change* (Chicago: The University of Chicago Press, 1954), pp. 4-5.

[46] Snyder, *op. cit.*, p. 467.

manner. In this beginning of treatment, the first interview, as the client pours out his negative feelings to the counselor, he experiences a release, a new sense of well-being which is known as catharsis. Although even at this stage the client may have an intuition of his sole responsibility to determine his life, the client may say "Tell me what to do," "Say something," or "What shall I do with my problem?"

During this internal confusion of the client, the counselor structures the situation; he refuses to commit himself by way of imposing his values on the client. Instead, the counselor challenges the client to make the decision whether he wishes to continue the treatment or not. This giving of responsibility to the client to search and discover his values makes him work out his own emotional disturbances and complexes in which he can arrive at a more effective and acceptable solution.

As counseling progresses, the counselee begins to make positive statements about his human condition and he develops insights into his possibilities for growth. As the client explores every nook and crevice of his mind, the counselor traces his past life as the accretion of events and impressions that lie deeply buried in his childhood. This tendency slowly and gradually builds up to lead him to understand and accept his personality.

In conclusion, in Carl Rogers' theory of the basic human encounter (non-directive), the individual reveals himself to another as he really is—stripped of the façade or the mask or role we often play in our everyday life. For beneath the surface of smooth public relationships and doing the things expected of us by others, present at the bottom in the core of the personality are the yearnings, the hopes, joys, sorrows, urges, feelings—the real self. Given a permissive atmosphere, acceptance of the dignity, worth, and uniqueness of the individual, man being basically good, will gain an insight into himself, thereby achieving integration of his experience, awareness, and communications.

III. THE ECLECTIC TECHNIQUE

The combination of the directive and nondirective approaches of counseling is commonly referred to as the eclectic technique. To develop this method the counselor has to have the experience and maturity to develop his own synthesis; it is to arrive at an integration of one's thinking in the midst of various theories; it is to make a stand on his will to change, his philosophy of life which is the result of a lifetime experience of counseling.

Proponents of the eclectic approach cannot be pinned down to one method because they maintain that there exist individual differences among clients. Methods and procedures will vary in dealing with different individuals according to their respective needs and problems. It is not the specific method or theory that matters. Rather, it is the skill of the counselor based on accumulated experience that plays a crucial role in the treatment of the client. This is the position taken by the exponents of the eclectic system such as McKinney, Robinson, Shostrum, Brammer, and Tyler.

Adrian van Kaam's Existential Counseling is in agreement with the point of view of the eclectic approach. The most important in the therapeutic relationship is the relationship itself. If the counselor-client relationship has warmth, care, and understanding, it does not matter what formulation or theoretical allegiance a counselor may have. When sympathy, rapport, and the willingness of the client to cooperate with the counselor are established, then the theories of the counselor become irrelevant. For there is no theory that can comprehend the uniqueness of the individual striving, suffering, thinking, feeling, and loving. All that the counselor can do is accept, understand, and care for his counselee. He may even have to throw his theories out as he listens with reverence to the revelation of another human being.

Van Kaam agrees with Carl Rogers that the client should be given a permissive environment to express his deepest sentiments. However, he disagrees with Rogers that the counselee can develop his values in any manner he likes. In Van Kaam's theory, the individual can only develop his choices and decisions within the framework of his history, culture, and tradition. Outside of these three influences, the individual has no authentic existence. Thus, Van Kaam's idea of assisting the individual in the solution of his problems implies giving of direction.

Furthermore, Van Kaam stresses the conviction that while the background, data, and other information about the client is necessary and valuable, the emphasis in counseling should be on the human encounter—in the dialogue between the counselor and the counselee.

EXISTENTIALISM

From the time of the Greeks to the present, the problem of philosophy has always been the problem of being. What is being? The Greeks answered that being is that which exists, anything which has existence is being, as distinguished from non-being. Thus, the tree, the chair, table, dog, and man are all beings.

The idea of being became the point of departure in Western philosophy because one would have to start from something in the being themselves. But how do we know beings or things? From the Greek philosophers down to the medieval schoolmen, we are dazzled by a neat, water tight explanation of the knower and the known; the former is the subject and the latter the object.

The subject is one who possesses five senses which act on the object, which in turn reacts to the subject. Pedro sees a man, with his own weight, height, clothes, expression, and style. Having his sense of sight act on this man, the object, Pedro then has an image of the man as he is, like a photographer who has now in his possession the thing photographed. St. Thomas, following Aristotle and the Greeks, held the view: "That nothing comes to the intellect without first coming in contact with the sense."[47] But this process is incomplete. As soon as the image is in the world of imagination, the intellect strips the image of its individuating notes that make it an individual man and abstracts from it the essential characteristics which it has in common with other man. Thus, the question: what is man or what is the beingness of man? The traditionalists say that man is a rational animal. From them they grasp reality by going into essentials, the constituting structure of an object, which is the realm of abstraction. To complete the process, man by virtue of his intellect, discerns a hierarchy of being from inorganic matter, vegetative, sentient, intellectual, angels, and God—resulting in a well-ordered universe.

In contrast to this old concept of being is the dawn of the new philosophy known as existentialism. This new school of thought criticizes the Greek philosophy because it leaves one cold, like a dry bone, in the sense that abstractions remove the juice of life. This does not mean that existentialism refuses to accept being: in fact it also accepts being. The difference between the two schools of thought lies in the fact that the traditional stops at being and its characteristics while the modern goes beyond and penetrates being. The Greek philosophy was interested in what is out there, its essence, nature, or reality. This paved the way for our understanding of the world, our subsequent conquest and manipulation of objects. The evidence of the

---

[47] Maurice de Wulf, *Introduction to Scholastic Philosophy* (New York: Dover Publications, Inc., 1956), p. 133.

value of Greco influence is very much felt in the socio-political economic structure and the advancement of science and technology in the Western world.

Although Greek thought provides the foundation for the present day achievement of Western civilization, it is also true that it laid the base of the ruin and tragedy of modern man. For the preoccupation with the object leads to the discovery and mastery of the forces of nature, but man, the subject remains a mystery, the unknown, the undiscovered self. Carl Gustav Jung[48] holds this view and he even predicted as early as 1914 the rise of the German nation and the epidemic that was to come.

The psychic epidemic did come in the form of two world wars. The European continent, the most civilized, the most advanced, proud of its rational orientation, became the scene of destruction; towns, cities, and industries were destroyed; millions were killed, thousands were homeless when order was finally restored.

After the two world wars, it becomes imperative for modern European to recast his thinking on being. It was to the two 19th Century unknown philosophers, Kierkegaard and Nietzsche, that the representatives of the postwar generation philosophy turned for direction in their philosophizing. Both men lived during the Victorian era and both felt the need to question the authenticity of the values of the society and culture of their epoch. Both wanted to evaluate their personal lives and on the bases of the evaluation establish a philosophy based on personal experience.

Soren Kierkegaard's[49] contribution to philosophy lies in his approach to human existence through the personal experience of man as being in the world. Philosophy will never be the same because of Kierkegaard's originality and insight into subjectivity or inward experience of man as the measure of truth. The implications of this methodology of dealing with reality opened our eyes to a new perspective in understanding man's relationship to himself, man's relationship to his fellowmen, and man's relationship to the world and to his God.

Frederick Nietzsche[50] who was of the same temperament as Kierkegaard and whose perspective and whose preoccupation was the search for truth in

---

[48] Carl Gustav Jung, *Modern Man in Search of a Soul* (New York: Harcourt, Brace and World, Inc., 1933), pp. 24-35.

[49] Kierkegaard, *op. cit.*, pp. 1-3.

[50] Nietzsche, *op. cit.*, pp. 115-116.

the inward experience of the subjective thinker was led to the conclusion that the affirmation of human existence is in the striving to be a superman. The superman is a destroyer of values, is above good and evil; he is strong but his strength should not be equated with brute force. This creature, the superman, scoffs at customs and traditions of society, especially Christianity for the Christian church has debased man, degraded man beyond redemption. Nietzsche's analysis of man's existence as conditioned by society is ruthless.

Edmund Husserl's[51] writings appeared on the European continent very much later than either Kierkegaard's or Nietzsche's. Although he founded the school of thought known as phenomenology, his thinking influenced the existentialist movement. Like Kierkegaard and Nietzsche, the approach of Husserl to reality was characterized by taking hold of the given and immediate personal experience as the starting point of philosophy. According to Husserl, man as a creature who can see meaning in things and his grasp of meaning can transform his life into a meaningful whole. This is possible because man is a being in the world whose "being there" can immediately perceive the being-for-me of others.

After Husserl, Heidegger's[52] name became a byword among university professors in Europe. As a philosopher, Heidegger possessed a formidable Aristotelian logic and he made use of Greek philosophy to arrive at existentialist conclusions. For him the basic problem of man is the forgetfulness of existence, when the individual is lost in the lonely crowd. In such a phenomenon the individual is involved in the trivialities of everyday life, in gossip and chatter, in the clichés and worn-out language of the herd, the common ordinary, vulgar massman. Heidegger is detailed, thorough, and devastating in his analysis that cuts through human existence like a sharp razor. In his view there two states of existence: the inauthentic and the authentic. Both are states of the mind: the inauthentic is one who eats, sleeps, and make a living and once in a while goes to bed with a harlot. He is a bourgeois through and through, living in the "midst-of-the world."

Authentic existence, on the other hand, is one characterized by genuine, spontaneous, and creative expression of oneself in the face of insurmountable odds set by society to make everybody toe the line. Authenticity means to be oneself and to return to existence. But what are

---

[51] Butler, *op. cit.*, pp. 440-441.

[52] Heidegger, *op. cit.*, 240-292.

the ways to authenticity? Heidegger set forth the answer when he said that man must do two things: First, he must have an awareness of his death: that any time he can be annihilated from the face of the earth. Only by contemplating death and accepting it can man awaken to what is essential in the business of living, the meaning of life. The second way to authenticity for Heidegger is poetry or spirit. This is understandable for a man who was influenced by Holderlin's poetry and who discovers pure being in the realm of that experience.

Jean-Paul Sartre,[53] leader of another branch of existentialism, contends that only man from his personal experience of human existence can determine his own values. It is man himself who makes himself what he ought to become. The definition given by Sartre of existentialism is this: ". . . By existentialism we mean a doctrine which makes a human life possible, and, in addition, declares that every truth and every action implies a human setting and a human subjectivity." And Sartre continues:[54] "Not only is man what he conceives himself to be, but he is also what he wills himself to be after his thrust towards existence . . . Man is nothing else but what he makes of himself. Such is the first principles of existentialism."

Rollo May, philosopher-psychotherapist, gives his view of existentialism: "existentialism means centering upon the existing person; it is the emphasis on the human being as he is emerging, becoming . . . Traditionally in western culture, existence has been set over against essence, the latter being the emphasis on immutable principles, truth, logical laws, etc. that are supposed to stand above any given existence."[55]

From the above description of existentialism it is not difficult to make an objective evaluation of the emphasis of this new philosophy. First, existentialism makes use of the human situation as its point of departure. Man and his world or man as a being in the world should be the center of the philosopher's interest. Man is a being, thrown into the world to create his own essence, his "to be." He is flesh and blood, has his two feet on the ground, a creature who has to discover his meaning through experience. It follows that existence precedes essence. Man as an existing being freely chooses to give shape and direction to his life. Man realizes his being a man only after what he does with his existence.

---

[53] Sartre, *op. cit.*, p. 10.

[54] *Ibid.*, p. 15.

[55] May, *op. cit.*, p. 16.

Secondly, because existentialism holds that existence precedes essence, it follows that man is a creature who is free to realize his being a man. The existence of man is such that he is capable of reflecting and transcending himself and his world.

Thirdly, since man is a creature that is conscious of his activity and can reflect on what he does and can transcend his environment, it follows that man must realize with all his powers that which truly makes him a man. Man is called to be responsible by giving meaning to his life, by choosing to be authentic.

Fourthly, existential thought is concerned with man's worth and dignity. It is ruthless in its attacks against the dehumanization and depersonalization of life. Backed up by painful memories and experiences of two world wars, the existentialist refuses to treat man as an "it," an object, a thing to be manipulated.

Fifth, the existentialist has been able to diagnose the problem of modern man as he confronts anxiety and guilt. The everyday routine and mechanized life of most men has reduced life to empty chatter and babble. The root of "angst" is the chronic suffering of being caught in the tension between being and non-being—the possibility of not reaching one's goal or realizing one's potentialities as a man. The existential school maintains that guilt and anxiety are part of life. Anxiety will always take hold of man's existence as long as man is not possessed by what Tillich calls "the courage to be."

Many studies have been undertaken to adapt the many insights of existentialism to counseling and psychotherapy. In Europe and in the United States, the number of counselors, psychotherapists, and psychiatrists influenced by existential thought are numerous. It is sufficient to mention the names of the prominent ones. In Europe, the leading figures are Ludwig Binswanger, Medard Boss, Roland Kuhn, and Rollo May. Gordon Allport stands out as the most outstanding. Since the center of interest of this thesis is on the existential counseling technique of Adrian Van Kaam, the researcher will now undertake to make an expository and critical evaluation of Van Kaam's Counseling Technique.

CHAPTER III

THE THREE TECHNIQUES OF ADRIAN VAN KAAM'S EXISTENTIAL COUNSELING AS THE CRITERIA IN ESTABLISHING THEIR RELEVANCE TO COUNSELING COLLEGE STUDENTS AS COMPARED WITH THE OTHER FEATURES OF EXISTENTIAL PHILOSOPHY

THE CRITERIA USED

Van Kaam's Existential Counseling Technique[56]

A. Human Encounter
   1. The Counselor and the client
   2. Self-actualization
   3. Self-transcendence
B. Freedom
   1. Openness to reality
   2. Willfulness
   3. Willessness
C. History, Culture, and Tradition

On the bases of the analysis of existentialism discussed in Chapter II the writer will now present the criteria based on the three techniques of Adrian Van Kaam's Existential Counseling as the criteria in establishing their relevance to counseling college students as compared with other existential philosophy.

---

[56] Van Kaam, *op. cit.*, p. 126.

VAN KAAM'S EXISTENTIAL COUNSELING

I. THE HUMAN ENCOUNTER

Existential Counseling begins with human encounter. The term existential comes from the verb "to exist" which means to stand out, to open to reality. Since man is the only creature on earth who is capable of accepting or rejecting reality, or use of the term "existence," "existential" and "to exist" refers to man's standing out in reality as being in the world. Counseling is a specialized field of study which enables a man to help his fellowmen to remove obstacles and blocks which hinder them from being open to reality. Thus, existential counseling is a human encounter because it is a meeting of two human beings: the counselor, on one side, and the counselee, on the other side.

Not all human encounters are counseling situations. When we meet each other in the street and greet one another because of long outstanding acquaintance, the nod, the smile, and the exchange of pleasantries is a human encounter. The stranger who stops us in the street to ask for a particular information on how he can get around the city is a human encounter because the wall and the silence that separate two persons have now been bridged by the sound of speech expression. The boy scout who helps an old man cross the street is another example of a human encounter. The teacher who does his best to promote the mental and personal growth of the students is continuously engaged in human encounters. The salesman, the baker, the businessman, people of other professions and calling are involved daily in human encounters. However, none of the above-mentioned example can be considered counseling situations.

Authentic human encounter is a counseling situation when a person who is disturbed and in despair about his anxiety cries for help from another person. The person concerned can no longer resolve his problems, he has met an impasse in his relationship with himself, his fellowmen and his environment. Life seems to have lost its meaning. The other beings in the world appear as frightening and threatening to his existence. The reaction of a disturbed person is one of constant fear and flight from himself. Instead of facing his problem, he wants to run away from life, from reality. But man as a great experiment of life has to be tested and evaluated in his performance not only to do what he can do but to do his best. So life as a process cannot just leave man alone to reject reality. Man is thrown into a situation where he has to struggle within himself whether or not reality is worth preserving.

It is because of this dilemma that the counselee or client goes and sees a counselor. The cry for help of a client is an appeal which the counselor must respond to. In the first moment of the human encounter between counselor and counselee is the initiation of the former to genuine therapeutic care for the latter. The counselee seeks help in his cries and pleas: "Please be with Me." This is the moment when the counselor, responding to the appeal of the counselee puts his whole self, in an act of self-surrender, at the disposal of the other. He has to shred off the mask or role he plays in society. He may be an educator, administrator, physician, theologian, or minister in his other mode of existence. In this very moment with the counselee, he discards the narrow, self-centered world of his studies, interests, and values related to his self-actualization. From his world of being-one-self, he moves to an attitude, an orientation as a being for others. In his capacity to do as a human being and a counselor he can experience self-transcendence.

> "Being a good counselor is therefore paradoxical in many ways. I exist not only for my counselee, I exist, also, for myself. I am also a presence to myself. Even when I am fully present to my counselee, I remain an 'I' a 'selfness.' But I remain only an 'I' a 'selfness' in my fusion with the 'Not-self.' For being human is a paradox of selfness and transcendence. The paradox of being man is even more dramatic in the therapy situation. Being a counselor is my being at the disposal of my counselee and totally dedicated to the unique personality which my client is. On the other hand, in the giving of myself and in the surrender of myself to my counselee, my real authentic self is revealed, actualized and expanded. This real self is best in men, my authentic 'I' which is at the disposal of my client, not the functional or social 'me.'[57]

Self-transcendence exists when there is a genuine respect for the client's uniqueness as a person. Like the counselor, the client occupies space and has his being in the world. His existence is characterized by his body; he is flesh and blood in his specific, concrete life situation. The reality of the presence of another man carrying in the depths and ground of his existence, his own share of pain and joy, success and failure, frustrations and triumphs,

---

[57] *Ibid.*, p. 33.

should evoke in the counselor a feeling of wonder, mystery, and awe at the beauty of man's freedom. Thus, the counselor tries to liberate himself from any unconscious motivation of influencing, coercing, and directing the counselee.

He sees to it that his lifestyle or values do not interfere in the counselor-counselee dialogue. The therapeutic presence and care of the counselor creates the atmosphere as well as the desire for freedom on the part of the counselee. Therapeutic presence and care has the healing effect of giving insight, meaning, and direction for the counselee to choose self-actualization. The counselee's response to the counselor's openness and spontaneity must be one of trust: both must trust each other. The counselee then must give his consent to work for integration in an atmosphere of freedom, free from any inhibition, suggestion, or coercion. This is an explicit affirmation and acknowledgement by the counselee that he comes to the clinic of the counselor on his own volition and he gives his free consent and cooperation. This is important because the therapeutic treatment or psychological surgery demands that the client muster the courage to take the risk of experiencing himself and his relationship with the world and his destiny. According to Van Kaam, once the counselee gives his consent and cooperation to the counselor, the former also gives his consent to be open to reality and the possibility of good that may result from such a venture or project.

> "But the therapeutic care of the psychological counselor can only be creative when the counselee accepts freely this loving concern. The 'yes' of the counselee is necessary to ratify the therapeutic concern of the counselor and make this fruitful and creative. The psychotherapist wants the freedom and transcendence of the counselee, and so he can only want the counselee to consent freely to the living care which is offered to him. Therapeutic care for the patient amounts to wanting his freedom. When the counselee does simply what he is told because of the fact that to him the counselor is an expert who sees 'through him' or 'is such a nice fellow,' the subtle process of enlargement to his freedom is still born. Therapeutic care is only fertile when the person himself who has to grow chooses to do so. For this reason, the approach of psychotherapy must be entirely different from that of medicine. Psychotherapeutic influence is an interchange between two human beings in which both are active and in which both participate. Without this free participation by

> the counselee, psychotherapy cannot be this 'yes' of the counselee as his gift to the counselor".[58]

The counselor joins the counselee in his project to search for meaning to grow in freedom and responsibility. He shows his therapeutic care and concern for the other by putting his whole self at the service of the client. He can not think of his own care, his interest, his own fulfillment. It is when he is fully engrossed in caring for his client, in self-surrender, in self-abandon, that later on the counselor fulfills his own need of self-actualization.

> "Therapeutic care is a most interesting case of this eternal human dilemma. For authentic therapeutic care wants in every case the interest of the client. On the other hand it is impossible for me as a counselor to forego the fact that my client is at the same time the fulfillment of my deepest being, understood as a being-towards the other. However, this does not mean that the actualization of my own humanity is the sole motivation for the living care of my counselee. The opposite is true. In therapeutic care I actualize myself only under one condition; namely, that this self actualization, this growth in human perfection, is not the motivation of my counseling or therapy. Imagine for a moment that my client were thanking me for my care, understanding and therapy and that I were waving it away by saying that it was merely a question of fulfilling my own humanity, of becoming perfect, or of gaining self-actualization. It would be immediately clear to my client that he is not cared for in an authentic sense but only in the interest of my personal growth."[59]

The counselor's presence, loving care, and concern for and in behalf of his client will uncover the meaning of freedom of a being in the world. Time is vital to the healing process, time is needed to awaken the dormant will of its potentialities. The counselor has to follow the gradual unfolding of another to discover for himself his freedom to will reality, to will for the truth, self-surrender and sacrifice for the sake of the other in the most difficult and painful experience of the therapist.

---

[58] *Ibid.*, pp. 56-57.

[59] *Ibid.*, pp. 34-35.

His patience and his time are taken up in exploring the feelings, perceptions, moods, and memories of the counselee. This exploration into the different aspects of a person's disturbed zone can yield a harvest of possibilities. In the first place, the mutual trust and consent to explore freedom and self-expression can unveil a new meaning for the client's reality and he will be conditioned to this new way of perceiving reality which is the consequence of his openness to freedom. In the second place, he will realize that the realities of life (the past, present, and the future) are not absolute forces that decisively determine his total personality. Reality is not a gigantic monster over which we have no control. Man and reality are simply there given or thrown in a life situation or man is being in the world. It is not in the position of man to reject or destroy reality; reality is a brutal fact of man's existence. Man can give shape, direct, and invest meaning to reality. Conversely, reality, whether man loves or hates it, touches and influences his existence.

II. FREEDOM

The therapeutic relationship between the counselor and the counselee, for Van Kaam, presupposes an explicit affirmation of the idea that the core of man is freedom. In man's existence is rooted the freedom to evaluate reality. Each man has to evaluate for himself whether the world has meaning and his stand to the world is the constitutive structure of his freedom.

This man, the counselee, has untapped resources, a reservoir of inner strengths and initiatives and undreamed-of possibilities. The "I" of the counselee is the source of meaning and existence. This is the reason why the "I" of the counselee is always referred to as the unique personality.

> "Man must conquer his freedom. The first responses which he made to the world as a little child were usually not free, but very much conditioned by the situations in his immediate environment. In the course of his maturation, he has to transcend increasingly this unfree aspect of his life, although this does not mean that he should reject all responses to reality and to people which he adapted in childhood."[60]

---

[60] *Ibid.*, p. 64.

The counselee seeks the help of the counselor because he is torn between freedom and determinism. He wants to break the habits, attitudes, and patterns of behavior that were carry-over of his past upbringing and conditioning in his childhood. More than anything else, he hopes to gain insight into himself and his unconscious and his conscious mind. He can no longer live the conceit and self-deception, the split between theory and practice in his life. The pressure of society with its roles, mask, and façade, as well as his own inner compulsions, guilt feelings, and neurotic tendencies has limited his freedom and openness to reality.

The step taken by the counselee to see a counselor is an event of liberation. Although he has still a long way to go for the resolution of his conflicts, he has taken a big positive step to set himself free.

This is precisely the idea of counseling. It is to help the client help himself to discover his freedom. In counseling situations the client is made aware of his uniqueness as a person by making him experience the dynamic movement and tension of life within him. By making the client free to reveal himself as he really is, he can re-enact, recreate, and invoke the ground of his existence as the source of his life and meaning. He will be able to evaluate independently his life and the meaning of the world as he sees it.

From the foregoing analysis of man's freedom, one can deduce that man has will, that man, according to Van Kaam, is a willing person.

> "If counseling, then, is a making free of the person and is an appeal to the freedom of my counselee, I could say also that counseling directs itself primarily to the will of the person. However, when I say that I, as a counselor, try to awake the dormant will of my counselee, I have to be careful not to use the term 'will' in an unwholesome sense, for the human will has been frequently misunderstood. When I distort the authentic nature of the human will I distort the whole of human life; for as we have seen, the will, the core of freedom, is the center of human existence."[61]

This primordial will of man, his nature, is what makes him basically open to reality. He is often called to have a dialogue with reality and his manner of listening to the voice of reality transforms his life in freedom and

[61] *Ibid.*, p. 70.

responsibility. The person, who lacks the will closes himself to the unfolding of reality and refuses to hear the voice of reality. When man's dialogue with reality is dormant, it can be the result of guilt compulsion, neurosis which can be traced to emotional disturbance. Consequently, emotional disturbance can be attributed to man's failure to integrate his perception with reality; it is man's incapacity to muster the overpowering forces of reality that demands from him the courage to face life.

> "To have a full, open dialogue with reality is to will reality; therefore willing is being open to the world as it manifests itself in my daily surroundings. Conversely, the lack of willing is to close myself to the appearance of reality in my life. It is the refusal to listen to the voice of reality."[62]

Van Kaam makes a distinction between willfulness and willessness. Willfulness is the abuse of the will which makes the will a separate entity like a push button.

> "In that case, we should not really speak about 'willing' but about 'willfulness.' Webster defines willfulness as being 'governed by the will, without yielding to reason; obstinate; perverse; stubborn; as a willful man or horse.' These qualifications describe willfulness as tyrannical and unrealistic, while its performance becomes increasingly isolated from other aspects of my human existence. Why is it that willfulness is tyrannical and unrealistic? It is so because of the fact that the will is no longer a dimension of the whole personality which is willing, but elevated to a principle all of its own which does not pay any attention to reality."[63]

And Van Kaam continues:

> "The person as willing, my counselee as willing, is first of all an openness to all manifestations of reality in himself and his life situation. A separate 'will' is simply an imagination. It is this radical openness for reality which makes man different

---

62

63 *Ibid.*, p. 72.

> from trees, mountains, and rivers; for the tree grows towards the sky, the mountain top pierces the clouds, and the river finds its way in the country without being aware of the surroundings, without taking any stand toward the environment; but it is the nature of my counselee to be aware of his life situation and to finally take a personal position toward the daily reality which he encounters."[64]

Willessness is a denial of the will and of real guilty feelings as a result of lack of dialogue between man and his reality. Willessness is evident in the client's life if opinions and judgment of the collective become the yardstick of his behavior. The drive towards conformity has a strong appeal so that he stifles the creative and spontaneous response emanating from the center of his personality. It is the characteristic of man who lives in this particular orientation to be boring to himself and to others; he lacks a personal stand, he has no ability to make decisions. A willess person has no authentic existence, no inner force and inspiration. He thinks that he is a robot or automaton manipulated by his environment. Consequently, he lives in a vicious circle trying to pinpoint the responsibility of his guilt and conflict to other people in his past life.

> "To be sure, we should not deny that man may be almost totally determined, but this is the man who has not reached the fullness of humanness. The unfree man is almost totally defined by public opinion, social acclaim, body chemistry, or neurosis, and has diminished his ability to respond freely to actual and past influences which he has internalized. He does not respond, but he reacts. If my counselee is one of these unfortunate men, he should grow to the conviction that there remains in him a possibility of taking some slight inner stand which will transmute his mere reaction into a response. Every time he does so, his responsibility will expand itself and grow in strength."[65]

Van Kaam negates willfulness and willessness as a framework for therapeutic cure. Willfulness or will power is tantamount to saying to the

---

[64] *Ibid.*, p. 73.

[65] *Ibid.*, p. 91.

patient that all he has to do is muster enough will to change his job, his environment, his religion, etc. Once he has made the adjustment or changed his outlook or orientation everything will be all right. The oft-quoted expression "If there is a will there is a way," illustrates perfectly the idea of willfulness. Van Kaam is opposed to this idea because this will just throw the individual to another set of reconditioning. He will pattern his life after models, goals, and values which do not jibe with his own rhythm. His life will then be drifting from one determinism to another determinism. Without genuine assimilation of values with man as the measure of these values, as he sees reality, man is deprived of his true worth and dignity—his freedom and responsibility. On the other hand, willessness can also be destructive for the client. The client comes from a family, society, and culture with a very definite set of values. From childhood to his present status he has unconsciously imbibed the precepts, habits, and ways of doing things in his milieu. His society decrees that he must submit to its practices and wishes. He absorbs the values of his society in the realm of his unconscious and he learns to comply with his duties and obligations as a member, following the dos and don'ts. His failure to assume a social rule, to adapt himself to public opinion, to social acclaim can lead to neurosis and complexes. All of a sudden he realizes that his life has been manipulated by people around him and he now begins to question the models which he cherished in his childhood. Looking objectively, the client as a human being becomes aware of his freedom. The process of education in his family life and community were simply taken for granted and accepted without critical reflection, and hence, were never internalized as his own.

III. CULTURE, HISTORY, AND TRADITION

In the preceding two chapters it was discussed that a man is being in the world, in his existence he is situated in space and time. Man is born into the world, thrown into the world to exist. In this regard, all men are equal. No man has the voice or the will to determine his being thrust into the world. The world is given, is there, and is the facticity of our existence. Man simply finds himself inserted into the world without his willing it. The world for Van Kaam is, for him and the counselee, the source of meaning.

> "As we have said, existential psychology sees the counselee basically as a relatively free being in the world. The term 'world'

> in this expression does not mean world in the sense of unknown, uncultivated, or bare nature. 'World' in existential psychology means the world of experience, perceived, humanized, cultivated, civilized, and celebrated by man; in other words, a world of meaning which is, for the great part, communicated to us in culture and tradition.[66]

The counselee has grown in an environment permeated by thought and feeling. The people around him such as parents, relatives, and clan provide the emotional forces and ties which constitute the cultural mentality. The reaction of the counselee to his group is characterized by sensitivity to certain values. The values and mentality shape his own behavioral patterns. The dos and don'ts of society are clearly manifested in his beliefs, prejudices, idiosyncrasies, associations, and contributions to his group. Human existence is always linked to the existence of a cultural or sub-cultural group. Existence has always implied the inevitability of co-existence. Man does not grow up alone in a vacuum. He has to be sustained and nourished by the most primitive state of human society, the family, before he can participate and be absorbed into the larger society and make his productive contribution to the cultural world.

The necessity for survival and self-interest compels man not to live in isolation but with and for others. On the other hand, there is another side of man's nature to rebel against the norms, structures, and institutions of his society. This other side of his nature is born out of the need and necessity to think for one's self and achieve his own self-actualization as an individual.

The conflict between man and his cultural world is a personality conflict of a counselee on how he can promote his own good and the good of society. In simpler terms man must look after his own interest, for if he does not, who will think for him? On the other hand, if man will consider his own interests only, just what kind of a man is he? This is a difficult problem to a man who is sensitive to the values and mentality of the people around him. The problem and the conflict it generates within the personality are full of pain and suffering. Just where self interest and self-realization end and where social interest begins is hard to draw a line for the counselee vexed with certain values that has ceased to have any meaning for his existence.

---

[66] *Ibid.*, p. 107.

It is here in this arena of the conflict of man and his culture and tradition that Van Kaam introduces a fresh approach, originality, and intuition into the problem. Van Kaam maintains that the counselor should encourage the openness and spontaneity of the counselee to have a dialogue with his culture and tradition.

> "While it is true that such a cultural or sub-cultural world of meaning is given to my client as an inescapable part of his existence, it is also true that it is not a dead collection of frozen and stilted situations. The openness which my counselees gain in my therapy should make him realize that his cultural or sub-cultural world of meaning is pregnant with possibilities and appeals, with clamor to be fulfilled, that the world is a domain of action for the growing freedom, not static but dynamic, a world of becoming. The more counseling fosters a real dialogue with the cultural world of meaning, the more my counselee will be able to take a stand and direct, to a degree, this changing world."[67]

Thus, counseling and psychotherapy is not just helping the individual or client have an emotional release of repressed materials in his unconscious and making them appear on the surface of the conscious mind. The concern of the counselor is to guide the counselee in making his own inward voyage into the depths of his collective unconscious which is his culture and tradition. The counselor's interaction with the counselee is not only meant to establish rapport, empathy, identification, and catharsis which are necessary and valuable for a successful therapy. In Van Kaam's methodology of healing the ruptured and fragmented self, he plumps into the depths of man's collective unconscious by challenging the client's dormant and unexplored "existential willing." Existential willing is the innate power and courage of the counselee to confront the values and mentality of his world. The counselee's existential dialogue with his world will bring about the revelation of the face of his culture.

It is a double-edged sword. On one hand, the dialogue makes man realize how this freedom to be open to reality is curtailed by the lack of openness of culture and tradition. He gets the feeling that his originality and creativity will be stifled, will reach a dead end, and will rot in the morass

---

[67] *Ibid.*, p. 108.

of tradition. On the other hand, he can view culture and tradition as vital, positive, and creative sources for his freedom to develop; they can be grounds upon which his freedom can have different possibilities of expression. In the first insight the counselee becomes aware of his dependence from tradition. In clear and simple language, this point of view was explicitly stated by Van Kaam.

> "Counseling should help the counselee in his personal existential dialogue with the treasures of tradition, for the truly mature man is he who does not make crucial decisions without a respectful dialogue with those who preceded him in the existential quest in the current of history. In this personal dialogue of my counselee with the customs and maxims in his family and community, his personal 'existential will' awakens. Without the others and without tradition he has nothing and he is nothing. And, therefore, the counselee should realize that the world in which he lives and the way he converses with this world are gifts from others who went before him."[68]

In another passage of Van Kaam, the author points out the dynamic character of both man's existential willing and his tradition.

> "But authentic counseling also enlarges the area of insight and maturity and therewith the freedom of the counselee and the degree of his independence of tradition. No amount of therapy, however, can make a counselee totally independent of the dialogue with past and present. Being really free and mature does not mean, for my client, that he is no longer essentially dependent like other people, but only that he need not lean exclusively in certain situations. Free and mature existence means, above all, that my counselee becomes severely aware of the limited number of situations in which he can thrust his own appraisal and of the more numerous situations in which he is compelled by his limitations to rely on traditional or communal wisdom."[69]

---

[68] *Ibid.*, p. 110.

[69] *Ibid.*, p. 111.

COMPARISON OF EXISTENTIAL COUNSELING WITH THE OTHER FEATURES OF EXISTENTIAL PHILOSOPHY

When we compare Van Kaam's existential counseling with other features of the existential philosophy, we discover that the other philosophers preoccupied with the interest in psychology have developed the same theme with their distinctive approaches and solutions.

The basic concept in existentialism that man is freedom was thoroughly analyzed by Kierkegaard. In his view, whatever man does is under his own control and determination. "Whatever it is, the idea that every man must make is under his sole control."[70] Jaspers, the philosopher-psychotherapist, is in full agreement with this theory. In Jasper's methodology, "man is an existence which freely possesses its own essence."[71]

This freedom in man is rooted in the ground of existence as a being who possesses consciousness, will, and reflection. Because man can be conscious of his consciousness, can decide his course of action, and can reflect on his reflection, he is a being who is responsible for the actualization of his life as a being-in-the-world.

Like Van Kaam, other existentialist writers are dissatisfied with the behavioral and psychoanalytic explanation of the nature of man. Ludwig Binswanger, an existential psychologist, strongly asserts that man is an "I am," not a consciousness detached from the world or reality. To talk about a counselor's relationship with the client is to treat the latter as a being-in-the-world in a dynamic process of becoming. This means that the client is in the world and has a direct and immediate relation to it. Binswanger goes further in his analysis as to what constitutes a successful therapy. The therapist must take into account the threefold relations of man to his world: the Umwelt, the Mitwelt, and the Eigenwelt.[72]

In Umwelt, the counselor tries to experience his client's experiences of his body. In Mitwelt the counselor explores the successes and failures of his

---

[70] Roger Traisfontaines, *Existentialism and Christian Thought*, trans. with an introduction by Martin Janett Kerr (London: Adam & Charles Black, 1949), p. 10.

[71] *Ibid.*, p. 14.

[72] Rollo May, *The Origins and Significance of the Existential Movement in Psychology, Existence,* with the eds. Rollo May, Ernest Angel and Henri Ellanberger (New York: Basic Books, Inc., p. 41.

client's human relations. In Eigenwelt, the concern of the counselor is the client's subjective experience of his inner self.

The above threefold relations of man and the world had its origins from Heidegger. Through these categories, Heidegger was able to elucidate man's existence. Using the freedom of man to transcend his situation, the Swiss philosopher was able to establish man's responsibility to strive to be authentic.

Rollo May is another psychotherapist who has been influenced by Heidegger's "man as a being-in-the-world." Man has a "there" in the sense that he can know he is there and can take a stand with reference to that fact.[73] The categories of Umwelt, Miltwelt, and Eigenwelt are also dissected as man's mode of relations to the world.

Another concept used by Van Kaam as a technique in Existential Counseling is the theory known as human encounter. This is an inter-subjective relation between the therapist and the client, the process of entering into the subjective experience of the client as soon as the first interview takes place.

Thomas Hora also is in complete agreement with Van Kaam on the theme of human encounter. Hora maintains that:

> The existential psychotherapeutic process can be described as a meeting of two or more beings in openness and wakeful receptivity to what is, leading to a broadening of consciousness through a revealment of that in which is hitherto has been observed.[74]

Hora continues:

> The capacity to be aware of the experimental impact of others upon one's self and vice versa, tends to open up a new dimension of consciousness, which leads to a growing understanding of one's own structure of being-in-this world or failing to be-in-this-world because of various defensive attitudes and striving.[75]

---

[73] *Ibid.*, pp. 86-90.

[74] Thomas Hora, "The Process of Existential Psychotherapy," *The Psychiatric Quarterly*, XXXIV (July, 1960), p. 499.

[75] *Ibid.*, p. 501.

Other existentialists have different approaches to the problem of human encounter. Sartre, who founded the existential psychoanalysis, sees human encounter in the anguish of despair and in the crisis of anxiety. "Hell is other people," says Sartre. This conclusion is based on Sartre's basic assumption that the relationship between man and man is that of a "peeping tom."[76]

Gabriel Marcel, on the other hand, sees human encounter as a genuine communion between persons to form a community. Man's existence without hope, faith, and fidelity has only one alternative open—despair.[77]

Victor Frankl's technique of human encounter views the role of the psychotherapist as elucidating the meaning of existence for the client. This is done without the counselor imposing his values on the counselee. Frankl simply opens and explores possibilities for the client "in widening and broadening the visual field of the patient so that the whole spectrum of meaning and values becomes conscious and visible to him."[78]

Finally, in Van Kaam's theory of history, culture, and tradition, he has shown his remarkable originality. As a counseling technique, it is compact, systematic, and consistent in dealing with the problem of contemporary societies—particularly the sub-groups or sub-cultures in our cities. Other existential psychologists are either vague or silent on the issue. Part of the explanation behind the silence of many existentialists on history, culture, and tradition is the fact that existentialism and existential psychology were born out of the ashes of World Wars I & II, the breakdown of traditions, and the alienation and uprootment of man from himself in a mass society.

Certainly, in such a situation, modern man is more concerned in restoring his fragmented self into a meaningful whole. Another reason is the refusal of an existentialist to go beyond the recurrent theme of freedom, encounter, experience, responsibility, transcendence, and other tenets.

As far as the writer of this thesis is concerned, only Van Kaam has shown a consistent theory of history, culture, and tradition as a counseling technique.

---

[76] J.P. Sartre, "Being and Doing: Freedom," *Essential Works of Existentialism*, H.H. Blackham, ed. (London: Bantam Books, 1965), pp. 309-313.

[77] G. Marcel, "Outline of an Essay on the Position of the Ontological Mystery and the Concrete Approaches to it," *Essential Works of Existentialism*, H. S. Blackham, ed. (London: Bantam Books, 1965), pp. 187-199.

[78] Victor E. Frankl, "The Spiritual Dimension in Existential Analysis and Psychotherapy," *Journal Individual Psychology* (XV November, 1959), pp. 60-161.

The two other concepts known as freedom and human encounter used by Van Kaam in his existential counseling as a technique are common themes explored, developed, and shared by other existentialists. This is one major contribution of Van Kaam to psychology. The other contribution of Van Kaam is his exceptional ability and talent to simplify and clarify the phenomenological, existential, and humanistic approach as a technique in dealing with the therapeutic relationship between the counselor and the client. He is so far the most readable on the subject of existential counseling.

THE RELEVANCE OF VAN KAAM'S TECHNIQUE IN COUNSELING COLLEGE STUDENTS

The writer, in the course of his research on Van Kaam's counseling technique, has met many college students having existential problems. The writer extensively made use of the approach of Van Kaam in dealing with the clients' problems. After two or three sessions, the clients themselves admitted that they experienced a power—a new sense of well-being that gave them the strength to cope with the daily stresses and strains of living. Having found their way, the clients voluntarily requested that the counseling sessions be terminated. The majority of them indicated the willingness to come back if they encountered difficulties and obstacles in the world that will prove no match or hostile or threatening to their newly-discovered ego-strength.

Typical of the existential problems of college students will be discussed in the following case studies.

CASE I

Anna B. is a beautiful and talented student leader in a local college. Outwardly, she is a success on the campus as an honor student and as an officer of the supreme student council. Everyone admires her—from the administration down to the faculty members and students. Without anyone knowing it, Anna B. has been living in a boarding house for girls and has not been home for the last three years. The reason is that she comes from a family with mixed marriage. There are eight children in the family and she is the third to the eldest. The father is a Catholic and the mother is a Fundamentalist Protestant. The eight children were baptized in the Catholic

Church and grew up as Catholics. The father was not a churchgoer and was not steeped in the teachings of his church while the mother was well-informed in her faith and in the scriptures. The father was very successful as a businessman but was unhappy with his marital partner because of her prudish outlook. He fell into loose living. In 1971, the wife and the children discovered that the head of the family was maintaining a mistress. This incident was a scandal to the eyes of his wife and with her influence, her knowledge of the scriptures, and exemplary role as a mother, the seven children severed their ties from the Catholic Church. Only Anna B. stood her ground and remained a Catholic.

She missed home and wanted very much to be reunited with her parents, brothers, and sisters. But she knew that at home she would not find rest and peace of mind; everyone in the family will gang up on her with quotations from the bible and they would pray to high heavens for her "conversion." The prospect of going home and being treated as a sinner who has not been saved was just too much to bear. The worst part of it was that her two brothers were staying with her in the boarding house and were always preaching to her about their religion. She was lost and confused when she called up the writer for an appointment.

The approach of the writer was first to establish a real deep and warm attitude to the client as a human being. She was made to feel that she was important, that she counted in his life so that the writer was willing to give his presence and time at the disposal of the client. The writer than let the girl talk about her past and in a subtle way, the former made the latter dwell on the present situation. The writer helped the girl explore the culture and tradition she grew up with and the possibility of her own reevaluation and reinstatement of the essentials of the wisdom of the ages. After three sessions, she discovered for herself the possibilities of growth and maturity within her Catholic tradition and there was no need to leave her church.

There were cases of similar nature in which the clients after their dialogue with their culture chose to stay outside the Catholic tradition and the writer maintained respect and tolerance for their decision.

Other cases involved ecumenical Protestants who encountered difficulties in the conventional practices of their churches. The writer's background and understanding of the diversity of lifestyles and cultural sub-groups (based on Van Kaam) helped the Protestant students to resolve their conflicts and the majority of them returned to their churches. These students were able to achieve personality integration within their respective religious tradition by their own reevaluation and reinstatement of the essentials of Christianity.

CASE II

Lino A. is a 17 year-old college student. In school his performance was above average. He was referred to the writer by his parents because they were worried about his sudden withdrawal from meaningful relationship with the immediate members of his family, relatives, and friends. The boy would no longer join the brothers and sisters at the family table. He became taciturn and uncommunicative, although he would respond to conversation when someone initiated or made the first move to talk to him. His rating in school dropped from above average to below average with failing grades in two subjects. At night he often experienced nightmares and he suffered from severe headaches and back pain. Three doctors had been consulted and all of them separately arrived at the same finding—that there were no physical bases for his complaint. He has been seen by a psychiatrist but the boy would not open up and cooperate.

The researcher made it explicit that he would not assure success or failure. Before he could be of any help to the parents, he realized that he had to meet the boy face to face. The meeting was arranged in the presence of the parents and afterwards the writer and the boy were left alone to talk in private, free from anyone's interference.

The attitude of the writer which was one of therapeutic presence, care, and love for the boy gave him the feeling of security, acceptance, and confidence. In subsequent sessions, he admitted that the genuine warmth and spontaneous sincerity of the writer dissolved his doubts and suspicions into one of trust. Because rapport was immediately established during the first meeting, Lino A. poured out all his frustrations, bitterness, hatred, fears, and suspicions that were eating him inside. He dwelt on the past and the writer let him do so as to establish the background of his present problems. He had an unhappy childhood because his father was cruel and domineering in his discipline. Being the eldest in the family, Lino was brought up to be always the model of his six brothers and sisters. To achieve the end of the father, the boy had his share of household chores—of cleaning the house, fetching water, and running errands for the family. Any deviation or signs of misbehavior of Lino was dealt with by inflicting severe beatings; he was also subjected to humiliation in the form of scolding and berating his helplessness and worthlessness.

After identifying the problem of Lino to be one of extreme hatred and fear of the authority of the father, the writer contacted an older counseling psychologist connected with a private agency to be the one to tell Lino's father gently and emphatically that he is the root cause of his son's predicament. Because of the father's love and concern for his son's welfare, he was able to take the counsel. As a matter of fact, he submitted to counseling sessions twice: the first to the counseling psychologist and the second time to the present writer. Today, according to the parents, Lino no longer has nightmares and does not complain of headaches and severe back pain.

CASE III

As a 20-year-old college student, Elizabeth K. is serious and intellectually mature compared to her peer group. She is deeply interested and very much involved in philosophy and theology and literature. She grew up in a middle class Catholic background and her childhood as expected was sheltered one. Elizabeth K. spent her elementary, high school, and college years in a college run by her sisters. She excelled in school on account of her talents and was a student leader from high school to college. Since the writer has moved around the circle of college instructors and student leaders, he was acquainted with Elizabeth's interests. It was in one of these small gatherings that the writer had an occasion to meet again the college girl. The group was ecumenical: made up of Catholics and Protestants from different denominations. Although the discussion was conducted in a friendly manner, there was a great deal of argumentation and debate on certain passages of the Bible. Elizabeth K. could not see the relevance of the clash of ideas and references. As far as she was concerned, Jesus was to be approached by love and not by quarreling or arguing as the scholars in the meeting were doing. Then she broke down, excused herself, and hurriedly left the conference room. A few minutes later, the writer, sensing that the girl was in deep trouble, decided to look for her and he found her sitting in one of the benches outside the church building. She was crying when the writer approached her. The writer was cautious and aware that giving advice or speaking from a book would not help the person.

He sat down beside the girl and with all the warmth, the sincerity, and genuine sympathy that he felt as a human being, the writer spoke to the girl: "Trust me, I am with you. Cry! Cry because it is good for you." Then she poured out torrents of emotions expressed not in words but in subdued sobbing and moaning.

After a few seconds the writer helped the girl to gain control of her emotions. The writer then put his left hand on the shoulder of the girl and he gently touched the girl's forehead for a few seconds. Then he told

Elizabeth to accept the pain and the anxiety of the moment because it had a message for her personal growth.

Elizabeth K. came to see the writer twice and she has been able to work out her personal adjustment with other people. She feels that her sheltered background has made her too idealistic and incapable of tolerance and understanding of other persons' limitations or deficiencies.

CASE IV

A girl 18 years of age came to the writer with the complaint that she found her classmates boring, her teachers uninspiring, and her lessons not challenging. She shunned the company of former classmates and close friends. She preferred to be in silence and solitude away from the crowd. Everyone called her attention to her sudden change. From a happy and well-adjusted girl she was transformed into a cold, aloof, and reserved person. She was once a student leader in the past two years and in her third year she severed all ties with student leadership and extra-curricular activities. In its place she became interested in books and spent most of her time in the library.

In the first meeting of the writer with Brenda Z. he noticed a unique personality that simply flows, glows, and sparkles with wit and intelligence. Brenda as a human being is a remarkable person. She possesses a dynamic personality that desires to be open to reality with no one to be opened with. In her own words, "her teachers, former classmates, and friends are phonies, apes and pygmies." She hated the inauthenticity of persons around her and the climate of mediocrity.

The writer did a lot of listening and guided Brenda to discover her freedom. She realized that she had to accept herself for what she was and that she had outgrown the values of her peer group. With that realization she was able to muster the courage from the core of her personality to dare to be different from the crowd.

CHAPTER IV

SUMMARY OF FINDINGS, CONCLUSIONS, AND RECOMMENDATIONS

SUMMARY

The major aim of the study is to analyze Adrian Van Kaam's counseling techniques and their implications to counseling college students. Specifically it sought to answer the following specific problems: (1) What are the important features of existential counseling techniques? (2) How do these features compare with other features of existential philosophy? (3) What is the relevance of Adrian Van Kaam's Existential Counseling to counseling college students?

The scope of the study was limited to the study of a branch of existential analysis represented by Adrian Van Kaam. It pointed out the counseling techniques, the schools of psychotherapy, and the philosophy of existentialism as the historical background of the ideas which ushered in the existential counseling technique of Van Kaam.

The methodology used was analysis using the criteria of Van Kaam's existential counseling techniques in three aspects. These aspects are the: (1) human encounter which considers "the counselor and the client, self-actualization and self-transcendence," (2) freedom which considers "openness to reality, willfulness, willessness" and (3) history, culture, and tradition.

1. In answer to Van Kaam's counseling technique, the important features are the insights of existentialism as applied to counseling and psychotherapy. They are dealt with under the three aspects namely; human encounter, freedom, and customs and traditions.

The important features of these three aspects are:

a) In human encounter there is the sacredness of the counseling situation—the encounter between the counselor and the counselee. The description of the process involved in both the counselor and the client is that the counselor must not seize the situation for his own self-actualization but rather make the situation an occasion to help someone in need of self-actualization.

   Guided by his attitude to put his personal resources at the disposal of the client, the counselor is able to experience self-transcendence. Self-transcendence is the capacity of the counselor to extricate himself from his personal interests and problems and by leaving his ego-world he becomes open and available to the presence of the counselee. Self-transcendence also makes the counselor full of compassion, respect, awe, and reverence for the uniqueness of another being.
b) In the concept of freedom, Van Kaam emphasizes that man is freedom, that is to say, his existence is openness and willingness to dialogue with the world and reality. The opposites of freedom are willfulness and willessness. In willfulness man is seen as unreasonable and stubborn in his orientation to reality. Willessness, on the other hand, is the inability of man to make his own decisions and choices because he has been conditioned to accept blindly the precepts of society.
c) The idea of history, culture, and tradition is a technique in which the client is helped to develop an awareness and openness to a dialogue with his culture and tradition. It is in this atmosphere of dialogue with culture and tradition which can open for the counselee the possibilities of meaning, action, and more freedom.

2. The answer to problem two on the three features of Van Kaam's existential counseling as compared with the features of other existential philosophy is: Van Kaam's existential counseling was also compared with the features of other existential philosophy. The other philosophers-psychotherapists are in complete agreement with Van Kaam's theories of human encounter and freedom. In other words, the works of Marcel, Hora, Sartre, Kierkegaard, Frankl, Heidegger and others have clearly shown the inter-subjective affirmation and validation of Van Kaam's existential counseling. It is in the theory of history, culture, and tradition

that Van Kaam stands out from the rest of the existentialists; the other existentialists are either silent or vague on the issue.

3. As to the relevance of Adrian Van Kaam's existential counseling to college students as the third problem of the study, the following techniques can be utilized:

    a) Human encounter as a technique in counseling makes the counselor meet the client as a human person.
    b) Freedom guides both the counselor and the client and explores the possibilities of their existence.
    c) History, culture, and tradition arouse the awareness of both the counselor and the client that becoming a person as a being-in-the-world has to be worked out in the framework of tradition.

CONCLUSION

It can be concluded that:

1) Adrian Van Kaam's existential counseling has three important features, namely: human encounter, freedom, and history, culture and tradition.
2) There is a similarity in the theme explored and developed by Van Kaam as compared to other features of existential philosophy. However, Van Kaam's theory of history, culture, and tradition differs from the other existential philosophies; other existential writers are either vague or silent on the issue of the role of history, culture, and tradition.
3) There is relevance in Van Kaam's existential counseling to counseling college students because his theory of human encounter, freedom, history, culture, and tradition are the suggested solutions to the existential problems of today's college students.

RECOMMENDATIONS

The results of the study prompted the writer to offer the following recommendations for further studies on existential counseling especially to college students:

1. Administrators, guidance counselors, and teachers must delve deeper into the Guidance Program of their schools to find out whether or not human encounter, freedom, and history, culture and tradition are integrated in the counseling practices of the counselor.
2. In-service education programs must be regularly organized to familiarize the guidance counselors and teachers on human encounter, freedom, and history, culture, and tradition as the new image of the contemporary college student.
3. The Department of Education should require that all schools offering psychology and counseling will establish the continuity of ideas, contributions, and relationships of different schools of psychology and counseling especially the three aspects of Van Kaam's existential counseling techniques such as human encounter, freedom, and history, culture, and tradition.
4. Masterands must be required to undergo extensive counseling and psychotherapy in order to make their counseling practice relevant in counseling college students.
5. The following ideas not covered in this research are recommended as subjects or points of departure for future researchers:

    a. Existential Counseling of Rollo May, Van Kaam, and Jean-Paul Sartre.
    b. The Implications of Berdjaev, Maritain, Tillich, and Buber's existential theology to existential counseling.
    c. The integration of behavioral and experiential psychology to existential counseling.
    d. The evolution of different psychologies to existential analysis.
    e. Marcel's influence on Van Kaam's Existential Counseling.
    f. The Phenomenological Approach of Merleu Ponty as applied to Adrian Van Kaam's counseling technique.
    g. The Comparative Study of Frankl's Counseling Technique to Van Kaam's Existential Counseling.
    h. The Historical Origin of Adrian Van Kaam's Existential Counseling.
    i. The influence of Secularization on Adrian Van Kaam's Existential Counseling.

CPSIA information can be obtained at www.ICGtesting.com
Printed in the USA
LVOW122117300113

317940LV00002B/487/P